THE DIRECT MARKETER'S IDEA BOOK

THE DIRECT MARKETER'S IDEA BOOK

Martin Gross

American Management Association

This book is available at a special
discount when ordered in bulk quantities.
For information, contact Special Sales Department,
AMACOM, a division of American Management Association,
135 West 50th Street, New York, NY 10020.

The text of this book was adapted from Martin Gross's columns, which
originally appeared in *DM News*. We gratefully acknowledge
their permission to reprint, revise, and expand that material.

Library of Congress Cataloging-in-Publication Data

Gross, Martin.
    The direct marketer's idea book / Martin Gross.
        p.   cm.
    Includes index.
    ISBN 0-8144-5947-1
    1. Direct marketing. I. Title.
HF5415.126.G76   1989
658.8′4—dc19   88-48043

Printing number

10   9   8   7   6   5   4   3   2   1

Contents

Problem Solver:
A Quick Index of
Innovative Solutions

To solve a specific direct marketing problem, check the list below. This problem/solution finder lists important concerns in direct marketing so that you can use this book as a key reference and work tool. You can also read it through like an ordinary text, and you'll find it a basic resource for ideas and new ways of handling problems that crop up in direct marketing time after time.

1 LISTS AND NAMES

Introduction

This book is for the working direct marketer looking for new ideas, techniques, and methods to improve results. It is a compilation of my columns for *DM News*, where I have explored ways and means of improving direct marketing results. Written for an audience of practitioners, these columns work to solve the creative problems that direct marketers face.

Today, direct marketing has embraced computer technology, sophisticated measurement of buying behavior and lifestyle patterns, and the communications revolution. It is a full-fledged member of the marketing team, along with general advertising and sales promotion. However, it has certain traditions of its own, which make it unique: measurable responses, targeted advertising, and a message built around an offer.

Some of the themes running through my columns reflect my

background in direct marketing and publishing, and a fascination with the process of stimulating creativity.

As my readers know, I enjoy studying old ads and direct mail packages. The valuable lessons of the past are remarkably contemporary in their application, and we can still learn a lot from the people who built our craft. This book is my way of thanking direct marketing for being so endlessly challenging and exciting.

My thanks, too, to Joe Fitz-Morris and Adrian Courtenay, who first opened the pages of *DM News* to me, and to Ray Schultz for his patience and counsel over the years. Colleagues like Len Reiss, Neil McCaffrey, Ralph Siegler, Tom Collins, Sol Blumenfeld, Bill Butler, Dick Fernandes, and Ralph Wemhoener have been understanding friends as well as dedicated teachers. I am grateful to Eva L. Weiss for her editorial encouragement and enthusiasm.

CHAPTER 1

Words to the Wise: Creative Copy Strategies

Questions to Ask Before Writing a Direct Marketing Package

Uncovering customer buying practices and habits is of crucial value in planning and creating effective direct marketing programs. Certain approaches may not work in certain markets, and each market requires its own motivations and appeals. A package should therefore reflect the patterns of the targeted market. To plan the best package, ask yourself these questions:

1. *What language do your prospects understand best?* Will they respond to elegant, understated tones—the style best exemplified by BMW or Franklin Library advertising? Or will they appreciate

clear, factual, L. L. Bean language? Or perhaps "hit-them-over-the-head" Publishers Clearing House selling?

2. *What buying appeals are most likely to influence them favorably?* Will it be an offer of self-improvement? Or self-aggrandizement?

3. *What are the most effective and economical ways of transmitting the selling message?* Are free-standing inserts in the Sunday newspaper the route to go? Or should you rely on ROP ads in the daily paper? What's better: magazine ads with bound-in cards or TV? If you're going into the mail, do you want a self-mailer or a jumbo package? Is a brochure necessary? Should you plan a lift letter?

4. *How can the buying appeal you decide on best be presented to fit the interests of your prospect?* Will an eight-page letter alone do the trick? Or would you want a heavily illustrated broadside? Will a telemarketing approach do the trick? If you're selling to business, should you plan for a personal followup? Do you want to offer a premium? Should you emphasize a deadline? Is there an opportunity for "charter membership" marketing?

5. *How is delivery to be made?* Can you feature promptness, free delivery, or a warehousing offer (buy in bulk and take delivery in smaller lots, as needed)? Is delivery to be made to homes, or is there a pickup arrangement at a local dropoff point? Will you charge extra for priority delivery?

6. *What are the service needs?* In the excitement of the chase, frequently the after-sales needs of the customer are forgotten. Ask yourself these questions: Will fulfillment and execution be a normal stage of the operation, or will you have to make arrangements for special customized services with an outside lettershop or fulfillment operation? Is there a complaint-handling facility in place? Will frequent adjustments be necessary? Are you offering a standardized product or service, or a customized item with endless opportunities

for hassles, hangups, and half-filled orders? Does servicing offer you the chance to upgrade sales?

7. *What kind of discount and credit terms are you offering?* In addition to standard arrangements, is there room for an elaborate and unique structure? For instance, is your product or service priced high enough to allow for monthly billing without a credit or service fee? Is your book club flexible enough to offer a deposit plan with cash discount?

8. *How important is your customer?* Customers are sometimes treated with an abruptness that is hard to understand, considering all the effort that went into making the sale. While we all appreciate the value of repeat orders, we sometimes treat customers as though they'll never be heard from again. Some offenders include:

- The magazine that only asks for a renewal, instead of making a house call or two by mail before expiration. They should be asking: "Is everything all right? Are you happy with your subscription? Do you want to send a gift subscription? Would you be interested in our sister publications?"
- The mail order company that drops millions of catalogs semi-annually and freezes out customers between mailings, instead of sending out smaller, targeted mailings on a more frequent basis. They should be saying, "Our September specials for our old friends." "Please sample this pre-Christmas offering." "Sale on slightly hurt merchandise."
- The insurance company that immediately turns into a harvester of premiums instead of a total coverage company. They should be proclaiming: "Our homeowner policyholders are eligible for this special on health and accident protection." "Open an IRA with your insurance company."

A few minutes spent contemplating the way a customer buys can pay off big for the direct marketer willing to ask questions first.

Six Powerful Headline Categories

Since 80 percent of all readers never get past the headline, it's the most important part of your ad. As the major element in capturing attention *and* summarizing your message, the headline should succinctly set forth the theme, concept, or main appeal of the ad. If you don't sell in the headline, you're throwing away four-fifths of your advertising budget.

Of course there are many ways to construct a persuasive headline, but the next time you have to write one, make sure you weigh these six approaches.

1. *Product claim.* A responsible statement (with supporting evidence in your copy) is a good way to capture a reader's interest. Use numbers if you have them. Endorsements work well, too.

2. *Good advice.* You can never go wrong offering the reader a tidbit, a mere crumb, of advice in a headline. A little suggestion that helps solve a problem or prevent it from happening doesn't cost you much, but can force your reader to move into your subhead and body copy. That's why smart book ad writers often take a good idea from the book they're selling and make it a headline. "Here's how marigolds can keep down insect pests!" (for a gardening book).

3. *Curiosity.* "Why aren't all investment advisers this rich?" "Are you throwing away the most nutritious part of the potato?" "What's wrong with this picture?" These are provocative headlines that can bring the reader into the ad, while preparing the proper setting for your persuasive message. You need not ask a question to arouse curiosity. By captioning a photo of a seemingly fine Volkswagen as a lemon, the writer of a famous automobile ad lured readers into his very effective body copy, which explained VW's quality-control procedures.

4. *Prospect selection.* Asking the reader to raise his hand makes him a participant in the sale, turning a monologue into a dialogue. "Do You Suffer from Sleepless Nights?" or "A Message to Asthma

Sufferers" select their readers. Tricky or irrelevant headlines may be a lot of fun to write, but they don't score very high at coupon-counting time.

5. *News.* While many products are not newsworthy, the good copywriter will try to find a hook that has a news approach, because newsy headlines command attention. "This Word Processor Wins the Olympics" has more appeal than "A Fast Word Processor from Acme." (The ad goes on to report on how the Acme word processor's speed allowed reporters to file stories more quickly at the Olympics.)

6. *Product name.* By including the brand name in every head-line, you title the ad for the reader, and, since only 20 percent of all readers ever look at body copy, you get attention that you may otherwise lose.

Using Screenwriting Techniques in Direct Marketing Copy

For the last eighty years or so, screenwriting has flourished as a genre. Yet, for most writers, it's still as alien and remote as hieroglyphics. However, the basics of script writing—preparation and plants, point of view and attack, pace, and tone—can be profitably adapted to direct marketing copy. They work well for TV commercials, of course, but also for ads and direct mail.

PREPARATION AND PLANTS

The screenwriter prepares you for certain actions or events, so they don't seem coincidental or convenient when they happen later. That way, you don't have to wonder, "Now where did that come from?"—which would disturb your involvement.

You can also foreshadow in direct mail. It involves setting up a certain story line or theme or establishing a plant (information) early so that you can bring it in effectively later.

Example: Ask a provocative question on the envelope—but don't answer it until you're well into your copy, when you've set the scene and established the credentials or authority of the product or service you're selling. For a book on insomnia: "Are you a lark or an owl?" Not a major theme of the book, but an interesting one that will come to light later in the package. Copy inside actually waits until page 3 of the letter to point out that some obnoxious people can rise cheerfully in the early morning while others can't gather momentum until the afternoon. This information is important to researchers on insomnia. And to the prospect—who is now ready to learn why and how this book can put people to sleep. It's not necessary to give the whole show away in the first few lines of copy, although you shouldn't forget to answer any intriguing questions you may have raised in a headline!

POINT OF VIEW

From which perspective do you want to tell your story? The omniscient, impersonal third person isn't necessarily the best. Many successful letters have been written in the first person, even though the writer doesn't have any obvious credentials or authority. It's a friendly, informal method of selling. Of course, if you do have an important person signing your letter, you may want to cash in on her name with this "voice-over" narrative point of view.

Consider changing traditional points of view. Why not have a first-person narrator for a catalog? Or if you're selling a work of fiction (as a book-club premium, for instance), have the letter written by one of the characters in the book.

POINT OF ATTACK

Where should you start the ad or letter? Just as a film writer must decide at which point to attack a story based on the demands of the basic story, so should the copywriter weigh the alternatives. A rambling story line may call for a beginning far down the line; a complicated product story may be attacked *after* the offer has been made. A story that tracks easily can be attacked earlier; a sales message that builds nicely can begin earlier.

Your attack need not always be at the beginning. For a video cassette promotion, you may start at some point *after* things have already happened, say, when the family has gathered around the

TV set to watch the new shows or when the cocktail party is enlivened with a description of the new movie.

A favorite technique of mail order ads in the 1930s was to present a problem—a social embarrassment, for instance—along with some friendly advice from One Who Knew. This was neat, traditional tracking. ("Do you make these terrible blunders? Then send for *How to Avoid Social Crimes.* It comes in a plain paper wrapper.") Then a bright writer got the idea (after seeing a movie, perhaps) of starting an ad at a time *after* the product or service had been bought. ("Just how did you know about self-starters? It was easy— this amazing book on Modern Automobile Skills had all the answers. . . .")

PACE

The speed and tempo of a film can convey excitement, thoughtfulness, oppressiveness, or drive. Long scenes with less activity result in slow rhythms, which develop a mood or give you a chance to learn about characters. Fast scenes can build rapidly toward a climax.

A leisurely letter with long paragraphs and long sentences can establish a certain high style or price range (if the reader has patience enough to stay with you for the entire ride). Very expensive tours or *objets d'art* can sometimes be sold this way. A short letter with choppy paragraphs, each paragraph a brief sentence, conveys an immediate, action-impelling feeling, and may be a good way to announce a sale.

But the good moviemaker intermixes fast and slow rhythms for certain effects, and the copywriter can do the same in a letter.

A long letter with short sentences has a drive and momentum that is often exhilarating. By the time you've finished reading it, your pulse is racing. The introduction of a new product or service can be helped by such a technique. A short letter with long, leisurely sentences, almost Johnsonian in their splendor, is an ideal lift letter from an esteemed publisher or third-party endorser.

Don't forget your audience, however. Impatient business executives don't have the time to read mini-essays; fine-book buyers study each element in a mailing package very carefully . . . and may even take the time to critique your sales letter!

TONE

The mood and atmosphere of a movie (lyrical, easy-going, forceful, florid?) are set by the writer's attitude and command of his material. A master film director can bring in humor in a film about violence and death. *Bonnie and Clyde* had amusing characters as well as frightening ones.

Direct marketing copy should have a tone appropriate to the product. The slogging, imperative climate of much direct mail can depress prospects . . . and sales. A sincere yet easy tone tells the reader that you are in command of the subject. For instance, you can sell a do-it-yourself book with style rather than the same old heavy-handed paraphrasing of the contents. Begin your letter with an anecdote rather than the usual "Do you know how to buy a screwdriver?"

A financial services promotion for a retirement plan had a warm, personal opening in its letter. Instead of the standard "Now there's a way to . . ." the copywriter chose to tell of a little incident that epitomized the need for this particular financial service. Sales ran 33 percent over the previous year.

For an open-end continuity offer selling an indefinite number of Western novels over time, the writer chose to emphasize the exciting characters and descriptions in the books rather than dwell on the rather vapid plots. Dialog and descriptions of scenery were intermingled in the sales letter. A careful use of cowboy slang made the promotion sound authentic. And a barely restrained enthusiasm (as though the writer had been an eyewitness) conveyed the drama in the books without overselling them. This resulted in a higher-quality customer who stayed with the series longer and returned fewer selections.

Borrowing the techniques of film can enrich the techniques of both direct marketing print and mail, and improve results "at the box office" as well.

Information Overload, and How to Fight It

With more than 1,200,000 newspaper and magazine articles, 60,000 books, and 100,000 reports published every year, information overload has become a widespread phenomenon. How can the direct marketer's message—advertisement, mailing, or commercial—get through this communications gridlock?

Let's look at the four most common problems and how they affect direct marketers.

1. *Omission and escape.* Recipients may simply ignore your message. By not paying any attention to your information—letter, ad, commercial—they withdraw from the task of responding to it.
2. *Errors.* Many people react to information overload by making mistakes. They may misinterpret an ad, fail to understand the order instructions in a catalog, or actually substitute a competitor's name while half listening to a commercial.
3. *Delay.* Prospects may put your mailing aside, intending to catch up with it later on, when they "have a chance." Or they may skip over your ad in a newspaper or magazine, intending to return to it the second time around.
4. *Filter.* A difficult or critical message is apt to be ignored in favor of one that's easy to handle. The complicated mailing gets tossed aside in favor of a self-mailer. The too-clever ad is passed by, while a simple one is avidly read. The complicated offer in a commercial is heard as so much noise.

If direct marketing communicators are to overcome the problems of information overload, they should start by studying some of the communications breakdowns caused by their own message.

1. *Lack of planning.* Has your mailing been thought through adequately? Is the offer the very best possible? Have you selected the best lists? Is drive time really the best time to air your radio spots? Is your ad running in the right markets? Are you timing your drops correctly?

2. *Semantic distortion.* Are your words sending out the right message? Is your guarantee too ambiguous? Your headline too clever? Are you too uppercrust for the market? Are you using an anecdotal beginning for a letter that should begin with a flat offer? Is your insurance mailing loaded with too many catastrophic words of gloom and doom rather than with a lacing of hope and promise? Are those high-fashion photos really right for a home-repair brochure?

3. *No clarification.* Is your message simply expressed, or have too many word processors contributed to the brew? Take the final draft home and read it to yourself without interruptions. Would you buy a used car from this man? *Suggestion:* Before showing your copy to the final arbiter, lock it in your desk overnight. Then read it fresh the next morning. There, aren't you glad you waited overnight? Oh, those omissions! And where did all those platitudes sneak in?

4. *Poor retention.* The all-or-nothing, go-for-broke approach has capsized more ventures than undercapitalization or faulty selection of markets. Basing all your hopes on only one mailing can be delusive. You simply may not have made enough of an impression. Why do successful direct marketers insist on mailing to the same lists over and over again? Because they know that poor retention of information is a serious problem today. You have to repeat your message several times even to be heard, let alone comprehended. So, if your first mailing to a new list doesn't do well, consider remailing it, rather than consigning message, market, and medium to the paper shredder.

5. *Distrust.* In a consumerist environment, many advertising messages—if not *all*—are listened to with skepticism. To build a climate of trust, send messages that are open and honest. Offer a firm guarantee. Describe the product or service with care. Note any possible drawbacks. Indeed, you may be able to convert these liabilities into assets the same way an ingenious apples-by-mail promoter did years ago. Faced with a harvest of still-tasty apples bruised by a hard rainfall, he talked about the succulent sensitive-skinned apples he was offering and the unique rarity of these

aristocratic goodies. The few complaints he did receive were from customers angry because they had received unblemished fruit instead of that extra-tasty bruised crop!

You may want to consider instituting a "communications audit," putting each message through a special analysis before committing it to the marketplace. This checklist may do much to prevent breakdowns in communication and help the recipient better understand your message.

☐ Examine the purpose of the ad, mailing, or commercial. Does everybody agree on its intent?

☐ Study the culture and environment in which you are sending your message. Are you speaking the same language as your prospects? Are you massaging their egos or are you haranguing them? Are you addressing their needs?

☐ Consider the overtones and subtext of your message. Are you insulting your audience by accusing them of doing something wrong? Have you priced your product fairly? Is your message one of pride or of promotion? Do you care about your audience or are you out to "sell" them?

☐ Are you saying something valuable? Are you going through the motions of the pitchman or are you genuinely trying to inform, educate, and uplift your market? Does your mailing give something away—a premium, free information, a discount?

☐ Have you followed up your message? Or have you cut off all links once the sale is consummated? Even a simple thank-you note with the package is a welcome communication.

The loss or distortion of information today is as much a problem as the loss or waste of energy. However, a little planning on the part of the direct marketer can keep the lines open and make every message much more productive and profitable.

Fifteen Ways to Get Message Action

Every now and then, behavioral scientists and psychologists will burst out of their labs with their latest communications studies. In their haste to share their findings with the advertising community, they're apt to run over direct marketers who are on the way to the bank to deposit revenues garnered from *their* psychological insights.

However, while psychological panaceas such as "fear appeal" and "subliminal messages" may be old news, other communications findings garnered from the study of learning processes can still be applied to direct marketing with good results.

Psychologists, like direct marketers, are fond of lists. Here is a summary of fifteen findings in learning theory that can help make your communications more effective. Of course, you're probably using many of these points already, but here is an opportunity to see them all set down in one place.

1. *Unpleasant messages are learned as easily as pleasant messages.* Watch your language: Your prospect may inadvertently get the wrong impression from your ad or mailing. For instance, try to avoid negatives. State as much as possible positively.

2. *Meaningful messages are learned more easily than meaningless messages.* Empty promises, ballyhoo, and pomposity will be quickly forgotten. A thoughtful promotion, based on the prospect's needs, will be remembered—and acted upon.

3. *Ideational learning is faster if distributed advertising follows up massive advertising.* A shotgun campaign may only soften up a prospect; targeted direct marketing will close every time.

4. *Products sold requiring mechanical skills are learned best if demonstrated in the ad or mailing as though the prospect were doing the task himself.* Time-Life Books' *Home Workshop* series was a successful campaign, thanks to the careful use of believable models who sawed the wood, hammered the nails, and painted the chairs. The generous use of callouts and elaborate captions helped the reader understand every step of the repair or refurbishing. The same thoughtful and meticulous graphic approach also helped to sell Time-Life Books' *Cookbook* series.

5. *Product benefits are learned best when presented at the beginning* and *end of a message*. While we're apt to automatically list benefits at the end of a letter, sometimes, while asking for the order, we forget that the prospect needs to be reminded of the reasons for sending away for the product.

6. *Messages that are unique or unusual are better remembered than commonplace promotions*. It's OK for a message to be unique or unusual, but not out of place or odd. Don't sacrifice believability in your search to make an impression, especially when uniqueness or unusualness can be suggested by the product or service. Looking at the product in a new way can give you an unusual or unique message that is completely natural.

7. *Rewarding the consumer who pays attention to the message enhances learning of the message*. Support commercials that give a lift to a free-standing insert, for instance, often reward the viewer with a gift for checking a certain box in the order coupon.

8. *Learning by consumers is enhanced when they are told the benefits they will receive from using the product*. A careful orchestration of the benefits will also always build response. Too often copywriters neglect their homework and don't investigate the product or service thoroughly. Result: A tedious summary of obvious benefits rather than choice morsels that make the product stand out.

9. *Active participation in the message enhances learning*. From tokens to scratch-and-sniff devices, direct mail can boost response by having prospects do more than fill in their name and address.

10. *Message learning is faster if previous or following messages do not interfere*. Use a bucket-brigade copy technique, building on the previous paragraph and reinforcing the message rather than contradicting it. Another successful method is to carefully insinuate a novel idea quite tentatively with just a word or phrase and then build on it, rather than suddenly present it as a full-blown concept. (For example, in the same garden products letter that may have

only been selling seeds and bulbs, you can sell trees as well, if you've posted sufficient advance warning by talking about the possibility of a little orchard *early* in the letter.)

11. *Repetition increases the strength of an older idea more than a newer idea.* A newer idea has the power of its novelty, but an old concept that's been around a long time—a negative-option book club, for instance—may need repetition to be sold.

12. *Messages presented closer in time to an intense need are learned faster than those presented when the need is weaker.* The advantage of direct mail—immediate, targeted communication—is nowhere more apparent than when it is used as a timely, seasonal message. Turn red-letter days into heavy-order days with do-it-yourself tax kits at tax time, gift catalogs before Christmas, or travel promotions at vacation time.

13. *The greater the reward consumers receive from reading an ad or mailing, the faster they learn the message.* A strong proposition and a carefully worded offer are the basic ingredients of a successful promotion. Why should I read this ad? Why should I listen? Because you've been told and shown that it's well worth your while.

14. *The less effort required to respond to an ad or mailing, the faster learning occurs.* Hail the 800 number! And the business reply permit! Make it easier to order and you'll get more orders.

15. *The more complicated an ad message is, the more difficult it is to learn.* Complicated mailings attempting to sell and educate at the same time, two-minute TV commercials crammed with details, ads that try to sell every product in the advertiser's line, all make a long winding road that no customer wants to travel. Keep it simple, and it's sure to stay profitable.

Serve Your Promotions Sunny-Side Up

Would you spend a dime to make a dollar? Would you spend a dime to *save* a dollar?

Offers can be positive, passive, or even negative. Passive offers are those that don't seem to promise anything. "Buy Now During Our Big Thanksgiving Jamboree!" "Announcing the Grand Opening of Our Main Street Branch!" There may be an offer, but somebody forgot to state it. Negative offers have a way of threatening. "Renew Now And Keep Your Subscription Active." "Don't Lose Out on This Offer Which Can't Be Repeated!" "Don't Risk Financial Catastrophe—Get This Health Insurance Today!"

By stating your offer in a friendly, positive way, you can attract more business. You also have more room for a good sales argument as you build on the warm promise of your headline or envelope legend.

1. *Make it easy.* It might seem a smart and fair idea to offer a "test" set of four weeks of a magazine for a special examination price. At the end of the month, the prospect is then supposed to tell you to continue sending the subscription for another eleven months at the regular price.

But the burden has been put on the reader to be both judge and jury. Few would-be subscribers are going to review for four issues before deciding to purchase. It's far easier on both subscriber and publisher to enter into a "cancel anytime" subscription without preliminary inspection. And you don't have to raise the hackles of the subscriber by raising the price from a short-term inspection offer to the regular full-term subscription.

2. *Make it upbeat.* An ad was tested with two headlines: (1) "How to Avoid These Mistakes in Planning Your House." (2) "How to Plan Your House to Suit Yourself." The second outpulled the first by 16 percent.

Another ad told readers, "Don't Swelter This Summer." The same ad ran with another headline: "Now Every Home Can Afford Air Conditioning." Which ad do you think pulled best?

One ad shouted: "Warning to Dog Owners!" It also ran with a second headline: "Keep Your Dog Safe This Summer." The second ad outpulled the first by 60 percent.

3. *Give rather than take.* If your proposition for a tour includes complete travel arrangements—hotel accommodations, carrier, guide, and transfers—at a 25 percent discount, you may want to make this offer: "Now we pay for your hotel room when you travel with us," instead of the usual "Travel Price Slash!" Words like *price* or *cost* say, "Pay me." If you have an introductory offer to a book club ("Take any seven books for $1 when you enroll"), give away the books and add $1 for handling. Or charge $1 for the first book, and "give away" the other six.

A smiling, cheerful offer takes a proposition out of the "merchant-customer" class and makes it an agreement between two friends. Obviously you are going to have to bring up price somewhere, but there's no reason your headline should always be a price tag. Look at it from the customer's point of view and see if you can soften the terms and sweeten the deal.

Delivering a Lecture in Your Direct Marketing Copy

Why not use some of the tried-and-true methods of lecturing in your direct marketing copy? A lecture is an excellent method of imparting information, because it can:

1. Inspire the listener to learn more on his or her own by infectious enthusiasm on the part of the lecturer.
2. Simplify a complex area of knowledge.
3. Provide a simple organizational framework.
4. Introduce a new field in an effective manner.

There are four effective characteristics of a good lecture that may be adapted to direct marketing copy: timing, styling, presentation, and evaluation.

Timing

The effective lecturer preassigns blocks of time to each of the three major portions of a lecture: the introduction, the middle portion, and the end.

BEGINNING

On the Podium

The introduction prepares the audience by providing appropriate background information, reminding them of what they already know, and explaining terms and concepts that will be used.

In the Mail

In the same way, a direct mail letter's opening can provide the groundwork for a sales pitch by illustrating and defining concepts in a smooth, unhurried way. You can give a clear definition of the product or service here also.

MIDDLE

On the Podium

Sometimes, the lecturer may find the middle portion of a lecture dragging, so he will shorten it.

In the Mail

The middle of a sales letter often tends to drag too. Consider your letter's middle as a connection between beginning and end, rather than a catch basin for all the stray ideas you may have accumulated along the way.

END

On the Podium

The good lecturer tries not to hurry the end. It is the most important part of the lecture, because it summarizes and sharpens the salient points of the argument.

In the Mail

The letter should not suddenly pick up steam after chugging along for a while and then race to a conclusion. Instead, pacing should lead to a logical climax with proof of what the product or service can do, and end with a call for action.

Styling

On the Podium

A good lecturer varies her speech in pitch and volume. She tries to talk directly to specific members of the audience. She avoids stereotyped behavior, like clearing her throat or playing with her eyeglasses. And she doesn't hide behind the lectern.

In the Mail

The good direct marketing package tries for variety. The letter may be written in a conversational tone, and the accompanying brochure may be more hard sell, with various graphic devices to capture and hold interest. Throughout the package, the same personality should be reflected, however, through style and vocabulary. A fresh phrase or a clever rewording of an old cliché, for instance, may enliven the copy.

Presentation

On the Podium

To focus a group's attention, a lecturer may use slides or other audiovisual aids to illustrate points and provide a change of pace. Audience participation is often encouraged by using role playing and simulation gaming. And a portion of the lecturer's time is often reserved for a question-and-answer session.

In the Mail

A good package includes graphics that forward the sales argument. Ask yourself if you want to shout or whisper, then select the best method of presenting your sales message. Be careful, though, to emphasize your sales message, rather than detract from it.

Try to incorporate such participatory devices as checkoff questionnaires or tokens to be put into slots. Other involvement devices are stamps and stickers, scratchoffs, lucky-number searches, and the like. And the order form can also ask the reader to participate: "Which gift may we send you for your order?" "Fill in the number of weeks you'd like to subscribe."

Evaluation

On the Podium

Good lecturers constantly assess their own performance, to see where it can be improved.

In the Mail

Direct mail writers should keep track of responses, not only to weigh orders or leads but to study objectively the strong or weak points of a package. Could the response be better if the envelope teaser were stronger? Is the lift letter pulling its weight? Should the letter be shortened?

Study the successful lecturer's presentation methods and see if you can incorporate them into your next package, adopting good timing, style, presentation, and evaluation.

Seven Effective Tactics for a Direct Marketing Message

Marketing and positioning are necessary strategies, but woe unto the copywriter who attempts to bypass the sometimes laborious but necessary task of getting across to the prospect the reasons for buying the product or service. Here are seven of the basic tactics direct marketing writers have been using with great success since England adopted the postage stamp in 1840.

1. *Present a one-sided message.* Your objective is to make as many sales as possible. Fairmindedness and equal time aren't virtues when it comes to selling. In fact, even mentioning the name of a competitor may raise certain distracting questions in the mind of your prospect. Proceed as though yours were the only product around.

2. *Arouse a need first, then offer the product or service as a means of satisfying the need.* This is the old "problem/solution" technique that has worked for mail order advertising for many years. It may be a need that has never occurred to the prospect before. "Do you make these tragic etiquette mistakes?" "Why can't you do quantum mechanics in your head and earn big money?" "Must you be silent when your friends are discussing Byzantium?"

3. *Associate the product or service with popular and highly desirable ideas or feelings.* Even a new need shouldn't be *too* novel, even though it's tempting to be innovative and use an idea that isn't immediately acceptable. For instance, claiming that piano lessons by mail will teach the reader to play Bach fugues in a matter of weeks is not believable. Years ago, before radio and television, music home study was sold on the appeal of "surprise and entertain your friends." Today an appeal based on the idea of self-fulfillment, or entertaining *yourself,* may be more powerful.

4. *Use an "anticlimax order" for consumers who have a low level of interest in the product or service.* Locate the most interesting argument for buying the product or service and feature it *first* when you are trying to sell to people who may not be terribly interested in what you're offering. Selling light bulbs to building managers by mail won't get you very far if you begin by talking about the advantage of light over darkness. If you can feature low price, quick delivery, and a free gift for large orders, do so up front, saving your weaker points for later—if at all.

5. *Use a "climax order" for consumers who have a high level of interest in the product or service.* Here you can save your strongest arguments for last, ending your sales message in a powerful call to

action. For instance, if you are going after subscription renewals to a popular literary or cultural magazine with a historically high renewal rate, you can begin on a note of humor or sidle into your sales message with charm. You can save your best act for last, with detours along the way.

6. *Draw a conclusion by suggesting the correct action to take.* Listing reasons to buy simply isn't enough. You have to have a logical conclusion that will summarize what has gone before, and then you should ask for the order. While the format and discipline of a sales letter will usually dictate this approach naturally (it's almost impossible not to ask for the order before signing a letter!), sometimes a brochure or flier just drifts off into a puzzling, indecisive final paragraph.

7. *Use nonverbal communications with special cues that elicit positive consumer feelings and emotions to enhance the product or service.* The right photos, drawings, and typography can improve results. A technical brochure benefits from a contemporary typeface. A booklet promoting a reprint series of classics demands a rich-looking photograph of a private library. Insurance sells better when photographs of a happy family accompany the text. And nobody ever bought a two-week foreign travel package that was illustrated by a portrait of the minister for tourism.

Should Copy Do More Than Tell Reasons Why?

While direct marketing has traditionally relied on careful argument and fact-laden reason-why copy, there are other methods that move buyers. These approaches should be examined by the direct marketer whose response rate has been dropping or who simply feels that it's time for a change.

• *Motivation with psychological appeals.* A favorite device of brewers and cosmetics makers, this approach attaches pleasant emotional connotation to a product or service. By creating a mood, you enhance the appeal.

A mail order health insurance program might include a brochure that is heavily emotional, rather than a logical, factual letter. The danger of financial ruin and dependency on others may produce an impact much more powerful than reason or objective argument. Incidentally, creating an emotional piece does not mean exaggeration or overdramatization. In fact, a straightforward, documentary-style magazine article would probably be more effective than an overwrought tugging at the heartstrings.

• *Repeat assertion.* A favorite of patent medicine manufacturers; in this approach a message is repeated many times so that a consumer will *have* to remember it. Again, if you avoid the excesses of some advertisers, a direct marketing effort based on repetition may work very well for a new shopping mall, an upcoming rock concert, or a trial subscription offer. (Why should an outside list be mailed to only once?)

• *Command.* A command promotion exhorts the prospect to do something: "Buy savings bonds." "Support mental health." "Don't mix alcohol with gasoline." These work best with products and services that are well-known. The direct marketer can use a command tactic by turning the usual sales target around, *starting* the ad with the call to action. Here's a variation on the usual TV commercial that ends with an 800 number being flashed on the screen: start the spot with a "command" to the viewer to phone the number on the screen, for the following reasons, and then go into the body of the commercial.

• *Symbolic association.* Linking the product or service to a particularly pleasant situation or person is a common motivation technique. In that same vein, companies with a traditional logo or symbol that people know and respect have a built-in positive association that should be nurtured. Abandoning decades of advertising and marketing goodwill for a new motto or logo is as wasteful as destroying a historical site or razing a landmark, and yet business indulges in it every day. Comes new management, a corporate merger, overreaction to a piece of research, or sheer boredom, and a favorite advertising device is shredded and tossed out.

What better way to capitalize on the efforts of the past than to evoke pleasant feelings? Without hokey nostalgia or self-indulgent business history, a popular slogan or emblem may give new life to a sluggish product or service.

• *Imitation.* Testimonials, status symbols, and spokespeople can stimulate action. A retirement community, a bank, a cultural event, or a pair of shoes can be sold on an emotional basis as well as with the carefully assembled body of facts so beloved by direct marketers.

Turn marketing inside out and upside down. Years ago, Campbell's soup was sold with rational arguments and long reason-why ads. Mercedes-Benz sells automobiles with long copy. Why shouldn't book clubs use spokespeople?

There are many different ways to touch the customer, through the heart as well as through the brain. By testing different approaches, you may find that the reason-why method, while still effective, is only one of the weapons you can use.

Attractiveness and Credibility as Selling Tools in Direct Marketing

Through the adroit practice of persuasion and influence, the accomplished direct marketer can often raise the level of sales of an otherwise undistinguished offer. There are several techniques for accomplishing this.

Attractiveness

An attractive package need not be an award-winning mailing to do its job right. It should be designed to establish rapport and communicate effectively. The point is to appeal to the prospect's perception of himself.

SAME LANGUAGE

The customer should feel at home with both words and graphics. Matching the semantics with the marketplace can offer an immediate basis for interest and action. An avant-garde layout may work for a mailing to art lovers, but it's debatable how effective it would be in a motorcycle parts catalog. Whimsical, allusive language may have a place in a subscription series for experimental theater, but not in a letter trying to convince men to send for a pair of mail order work shoes.

LIKABILITY

Projecting friendship and empathy is more than saying "I like you." Both the message and the tone must be friendly, without being ingratiating. Lacking instant feedback, the direct marketer has to convey an impression that will instantly strike the right chord with the prospect. An empathetic approach will help you avoid false notes that can hurt an otherwise worthwhile offer: A needlessly complicated mailing that's hard to understand. Eight-point type in a mailing to senior citizens. Copy that is vain and self-centered. The commercial that uses loud or amateurish announcers.

The most successful copywriters employ a technique that direct marketing expert Leonard Reiss calls "sweet reason." Buttressed by facts, this copy method converses with the prospect, convincing him by example and precise language to send in the coupon today. Furthermore, the good feelings stay with the customers, so that, in the case of a two-step effort, for instance, they are more likely to write a check or sign a contract or enroll in a course, even though the action called for may be several weeks after the original contract.

Credibility

What do your prospects think of your trustworthiness and expertise? Do they believe your promises of quality? Are they thronging to subscribe to a magazine they never heard of before? Are they calling your 800 number to order a new kind of insurance? Are they voting for your candidate?

Building high credibility isn't always a matter of throwing in a couple of testimonials and a spec sheet. It calls for a careful analysis of your market.

For instance, an offer aimed at young intellectuals—a subscription, perhaps—has to be designed differently from an offer to record-club members. Their ages may overlap, there may even be some young intellectuals in the record club, and on the whole the record-club members may have more discretionary income, but there's a sharp difference in the thrust needed.

Young record-club members are "other-directed." They have idols and heroes. They look to others for leadership. They're more sensitive to what people think. And they're more likely to be susceptible to trends and social influences. Copy and art have to be contemporary, fast-paced, hard-line. Credibility for this prospect lies in identification with the service and its attractiveness.

The inner-directed prospect for a thoughtful newsletter, on the contrary, looks toward the perceived expertise of the contributors and how their ideas match her own. If the promotion, mailing, ad, or commercial is correctly presented, this kind of prospect will come away respecting the trustworthiness of the seller. The presentation need not be dull. It can be—must be—exciting, but it must exude veracity.

Attractiveness and credibility are powerful, sophisticated selling tools. When positioned correctly, they can provide surrogate sales power as your ambassador in the marketplace.

How to Be a Well-Rounded Copywriter

Mastering one form of direct market copywriting is hard enough, but *three* sounds impossible. However, if your copy is to work effectively under all sorts of conditions, you need to be versatile.

There are many kinds of copywriters, but they can probably be roughly categorized as belonging to one of the following three schools: closers, missionaries, and educators. See which category you would presently place yourself in and consider the advantages of being able to think and write with equal ability in other genres.

CLOSERS

The closer writes brief, tight copy. Sentences are terse. Paragraphs are no more than two or three sentences long. Letters are only one page, with incomplete sentences, phrases, and even one- or two-word chunks scattered throughout. For this writer, the short personalized message, imitation memo, or postcard are also ideal media. Often called on to write publisher's letters, this copywriter excels in broadcast copy, both TV and radio, and also has a feeling for the clipped, staccato pacing that a mailgram requires. A sense of urgency permeates the closer's prose. Art directors like to work with closers, since there is rarely a problem with long copy. Photo captions are just succinct phrases, and headlines and envelope legends, although sometimes cryptic in their brevity, have a drive that pulls the reader into the copy. Occasionally a crossover from general advertising, the closer has a style in synch with today's hurried nonreaders.

The closer is often the slowest writer of the three, because of the "less is more" need to cut and cut again. This writer's spare style is sometimes criticized for its lack of detail, but every word is measured and works very hard. Especially good for executives and youth markets.

EDUCATORS

Educators weave a special magic with "how-to" books, catalogs, and difficult subjects. They can make financial products understandable—and sell them. Unhappy with the skimpiness that anything less than three pages gives them, they write magnificent brochures. Expensive products—real estate, cars, travel—come alive in their prose. The two-minute television commercial is barely long enough for them to demonstrate the product, sell it, and repeat the message. (They are great repeaters.) Their ads (in very small type) have made millions for generations of mail order firms. Indeed, in the heyday of long copy, these were the direct marketing kings. They developed marketing strategy, penciled rough layouts, and even chose lists and media. Today, they are used successfully to introduce new products and concepts, promote continuity programs, and raise funds.

MISSIONARIES

Missionaries have a need to convert everyone and they don't let go until they've made a sale. Look for them to design the "layered" direct mail package, with each layer attempting to make the sale: The exciting envelope with a benefit, an offer, and a contest announcement forcing readers to go inside. The letter with a postscript that may extend for a half page, with a message so sincere and heartfelt that even cynics will read it to the end—and act on it. An order card that is a billboard, with strong selling copy (an opportunity sometimes not taken advantage of by other writers). A brochure that takes the reader by the hand and excitedly points out the advantages and features and benefits in a way that throws new light on the product. They will toss in a sealed envelope with still another message, and a publisher's letter that turns that austere executive into a pitchman. They write humorless, persuasive radio commercials for financial products, and they produce evocative TV spots for charities. Use them for insurance products in print.

You can see the strengths and weaknesses of each type of writer (exaggerated here.) The important thing to remember is that no writer should be limited to one particular style or method of selling. Using a closer style in an educator package may be a powerful way to sell to a market that's getting a little tired. Using the fervor of a missionary communicator in an otherwise cool medium may make the message jump out in front of all the competition. While writers may classify themselves one way or the other, the lines between categories do blur, and there's no harm in having more than one style to call upon.

An Underused Way to Guarantee Fund-Raising Success

While guarantees are not usually thought of when designing a fund-raising strategy, they can provide a persuasive twist.

As the for-profit sector of direct marketing has long known, a guarantee is reassuring. It's the vendor's promise of quality and satisfaction. It may not be possible to promise a cash refund if the subscriber is not satisfied, but the fund raiser can still use various kinds of guarantee offers as effective closers.

A charity can make a nothing-up-our-sleeves unconditional guarantee, using a copy of an audited statement or a notarized pledge by an officer. This unconditional guarantee might take the form of a lift letter (an addition to a mailing that lifts response) or an impressive certificate.

An attestation of policy, sometimes called "A Contributor's Bill of Rights," may also be included, noting that the particular charity subscribes to the ethical standards of a national organization, or has been checked by a regulatory body and approved, or that all the money harvested through the appeal is devoted to good works. A certified public accountant's financial imprimatur is also reassuring, especially if there's been some bad press about expensive fundraising procedures, with only a tiny portion of donations going back to the charity.

A third-party guarantee could also be used, such as an approval of the charity by an outside group or personality. For instance, an endorsement by a celebrity or a reprint of a feature on the charity from a nationally distributed periodical is reassuring.

If two similar organizations—the Boy Scouts and the PAL, for instance, or two veterans groups—are vying for the same dollar, a competitive guarantee may tip the scales. "If you feel that the other charity is doing a better job, let us know. We'll investigate, and, if you're right, we'll make a matching-dollar contribution to the other fellow." This is a daring and somewhat desperate tactic, probably best for a charity that has been suffering erosion from competitors and has nothing to lose by naming names. (Most charitable appeals sound as though they have the franchise for the particular misery under consideration.)

A device that is really a guarantee, though not usually thought of as one, is the "gift of love" offer that accompanies unordered gifts. Whether it's a sheet of address labels or a key ring, the premium is meant to be kept by the prospect, although you are left with the impression that a lot of children will go to sleep hungry because you've pocketed the handcrafted vinyl bookmark without writing a check. The guarantee here is a tacit statement of the fund raiser's faith in humanity. This technique has been overused in the past, and is semi-retired, but may be due for a revival.

Dramatized guarantees are considered unsophisticated and are best reserved for last-ditch appeals. These can take the form of copies of notices of impending sheriff's sales, collection notices from vendors (usually heating oil or utilities), or eviction notices. The guarantee here is that the need is very real. Public TV stations are not above programming taped college lectures on pre-Raphaelite art or documentaries on Lithuanian basketball during fund drives, again with the unspoken suggestion that this is all you'll be getting unless you respond to the appeal.

The double-your-money-back refund guarantee has its counterpart in not-for-profit DM—the matching dollar program. This can be very effective, especially when linked to another guarantee: the limited-time offer. In commercial usage, a limited-time offer says: "Your money cheerfully refunded if product returned within seven days." In fund raising, the limited-time offer ties the matching dollar program to a deadline. Or to a number of deadlines, in the case of a Dutch auction: a contributed dollar is matched equally when received by a certain date, matched by 50 percent when received two weeks later, only 25 percent a month later, and so on.

Fund raising, like all direct marketing, requires consumer benefits. A guarantee-like tactic underwrites the most important consumer benefit of all in fund raising: that the contribution is going to a worthwhile cause.

Using the Hidden Meanings of Language

Subliminal meanings, long the subject of psycholinguistic scholarship, have intrigued advertising people as well. Ever since the days of general semantics, when Alfred Korzybski, Stuart Chase, and S. I. Hayakawa plumbed the depths of significance to show us that language carried many messages, marketers have tried to harness the unspoken meaning of words.

In certain areas of direct marketing these silent messages can play a significant role. Once communicators realize that what they are saying may not be what their listeners are hearing, the possibilities for communicating many messages are unlimited.

TIRED LANGUAGE

Lazy language, old hand-me-down phrases, and clichés can indicate several things to a prospect. In a letter promoting a wonder of technology, such as a video cassette recorder or a computer, boring phrases like "You have to see it to believe it!" (always punctuated with an exclamation point) signify the writer's lack of knowledge or interest.

A stereotyped illustration is a graphic form of tired language. A stock photo of a happy family on a beach for a travel folder nicely fills up space, but does nothing to forward the sales argument. On the other hand, a stock photo of a happy family in a mail order health insurance brochure isolates and dramatizes the prime reason for taking the insurance.

One way of enlivening a mailing is to give an old cliché a new twist. "They say it couldn't be done . . . and they were right" for a book on the Edsel auto. "Leap before you look" for a book on parachutists.

UNIMMEDIATE IMPACT

Using the third person has long been known to direct marketers as a means of "distancing" seller from buyer. It's not only impersonal, it's vaguely insulting. Remote and unsociable, the third person has never been a favorite character in direct marketing scripts.

Using the second person in letters is as conventional by now as signing letters with blue ink. The *you* grabs the reader's attention. It's flattering, and it brings him right into the action.

However, the use of the first person should not be overlooked in letters. It is often avoided because it may sound like bragging, but it can be a powerful sales tool when used judiciously. Mark its use in "buck slips"—the little notes that pick up on a theme and say to the reader: "Frankly, I don't understand why more people don't respond to our subscription offer." The first person rules in these little "pick-me-ups," perhaps because of its informality. And that same informal tone when used in the main sales letter can work wonders. It can cajole, inspire, seduce, reveal—in a way that the *you* cannot.

OVERKILL

Hyperbole and hot air are not as prominent in sales literature as they once were. However, you can still find startlingly irrelevant copy in a lot of direct mail.

Next time you're tempted to parade all the testimonials in your file or crow about every specification, think of the consumers. Are you answering their questions? Are you listening to them? Or are you just talking too much (and injuring your chances for a sale)?

That very elaborate brochure for a continuity series: is it a bit frantic in its promises? The full-page ad for the do-it-yourself book: will the book really do away with contractors and handymen? The 120-second exercise machine TV commercial: will the device really melt flab and build sinews?

Hot air not only sends up a signal of possible distress, it signifies to prospects that the vendor doesn't exactly value their judgment.

There are many levels of communication in direct marketing. From printed word to unspoken hints, each level should work at getting the order.

Climbing the Seven Steps of a Direct Marketing Sale

The oldest direct mail copy formula around—"AIDA"—has been with us for so long that we may have forgotten where it originated. Actually, it came from *selling*. It was 1925 when E. K. Strong, in his book *The Psychology of Selling*, first proposed this formula for salesmanship. He said that, in order for the salesman to move the prospect through the phases of buying readiness, it was necessary to: "A, get Attention; I, arouse Interest; D, stimulate Desire; A, ask for Action."

Like Strong, many commentators have analyzed the selling process and have broken its stages into separate and discrete steps.

This analysis of personal selling lends itself to the creation of an effective model for direct marketing selling.

STEP 1: PROSPECTING

Using several techniques, salespeople look for prospective customers, those who are qualified to buy. In "the snowball approach"—which direct marketers have adapted into "the member-get-a-member approach"—satisfied customers recommend other names. The traditional "lead-generation" strategy—ads and mailings designed to build up a body of names the salesperson can "work"—has been used in direct marketing since the very beginning of the industry. In fact, lead generation itself is a traditional direct marketing process, involving a *two-step approach*; first obtain the names of prospects through an offer, and then try to make the sale through a followup. The least effective selling method is the "cold-canvas approach" where a salesperson blindly calls on a number of people, knowing very little about them. This is equivalent to buying space in a publication on the strength of its catchy name or using a list just because it's cheap. The amount of time and effort expended in this unplanned selling will outweigh any benefits.

STEP 2: PREAPPROACH

Good salespeople spend some time at their desk before going out to meet the prospect. They analyze any information they have about the prospect's past purchasing habits, including recency, frequency, and average purchase size. They study the prospect's current needs. And they productively brood about the competition. Direct marketers work the same way. They design an approach strategy by assessing the market, researching the product or service for benefits, studying any alternatives the competition may offer, choosing media and lists, and creating an offer.

STEP 3: THE APPROACH

What happens when salespeople meet their prospect? If they haven't done their homework, they'll probably never be able to secure the buyer's interest and attention. However, if an imaginative entry (based on an analysis of the prospect's working environment) gets them past the secretary, the ringing phones, and all the other bids for attention, they have a good chance of succeeding. The direct mail effort that doesn't stand out in the morning mail, the ad that is easy to overlook, the commercial that is silly or poorly produced or emanates a barely discernible energy level are all ineffective sales approaches that virtually eliminate any chance of success.

STEP 4: THE PRESENTATION

Here, the task is to tell as complete a story as possible about the product's attributes and benefits. In a short time, salespeople have to gain the prospect's confidence and change his behavior. Whether they serve as order taker, order getter, or missionary building goodwill for a more intensive selling effort later on, salespeople will be attempting to send out an effective message, which must be spontaneous and flexible.

The effective direct marketing message must also have this feeling of spontaneity and flexibility. Personalized direct mail, warm *you* copy in print, or a benefits-rich commercial go a long way toward achieving this goal, and a good direct marketer is deservedly called a "salesperson in print."

STEP 5: MEETING OBJECTIONS

When you're face-to-face or on the phone with a prospect, you can overcome objections and turn them aside. Effective salespeople can even turn objections into reasons for buying their product or service.

Except in telemarketing, you don't have this luxury in direct marketing, so you have to anticipate blockages and indecision. You can do this with a fully informative presentation that leaves nothing to chance; a seemingly ingenuous approach that actually lists possible objections and gracefully turns them into reasons to buy (much favored in the mail order insurance business); and a strong guarantee, sampling offer, or free trial. If you have a telemarketing effort in place, then you may want to tell your prospects to call for more information if they have any questions.

STEP 6: CLOSING THE SALE

Able salespeople know when to shut up and ask for the order. Those who can't seem to close are known as "conversationalists." While you can't monitor verbal and body language of your prospect the way a good salesperson can face-to-face, you can build an environment where you get the prospect to commit then and there. Adroitly marshall your sales argument with good persuasive copy, ask for the order early in the game with a "trial close" (impatient readers quick to understand the message will appreciate the opportunity you offer them to get on with it), and leave no exit for indecision. Incidentally, the careful use of deadlines and discounts can often demolish delays in ordering.

STEP 7: FOLLOWUP

This important tool in personal selling is so often neglected in direct marketing. Checking with buyers to see if they're happy with the purchase and getting full utility from it is second nature with salespeople, and it should also be a part of direct marketing. Followup offers the chance to suggest add-on sales, sell maintenance items, and procure names of other prospects. Buyers are ready to increase their investment to gain more advantages from the initial buy, are committed to a relationship with the seller, and are as warm and friendly as they'll ever be. And if they've made a substantial outlay in the purchase, they may want more information to buttress their decision and rationalize the purchase. Psychologists call this step "preventing dissonance"; direct marketers call it building a customer list.

By using the strategies and tactics of personal selling, direct marketers can often encourage the formation of a buying decision in a person they may never meet face-to-face but who has been communicated with directly and effectively.

The Art of Persuasion: Aristotle's Guide to Classic Style

Aristotle's three qualities of effective style—clarity, appropriateness, and vividness—have particular meaning for direct marketing writers, because he was primarily concerned with the art of persuasion.

Three Classic Tools

CLARITY

As a writer, you're once removed from the consumer and you have only one chance to present your message. If your copy is obscure or uncertain, you don't have a chance to clarify your meaning.

The good copywriter surrounds a possibly ambiguous term with enough context to clarify its intended meaning. So, instead of just saying "The car can be leased very easily," explain that the car can be leased from the XYZ Company. List available car makes. And show how freedom from paperwork makes leasing from the XYZ Company so easy.

By using concrete words, you yield more information and accuracy, carefully moving your prospect over to your way of thinking by sharing facts. An author isn't merely a "good" writer. She's "witty" or a "gifted master of social comedy." The tie isn't just "made" of silk. It's carefully "woven," usually by dexterous craftsmen plying their ancient skill. Use descriptive verbs. Not "ran quickly," but "sprinted."

Avoid unfamiliar words if possible; they convey no information. However, if you do need to use an unfamiliar word, define it carefully, thus giving the prospect a sense of instant expertise.

APPROPRIATENESS

Make sure your style is appropriate to your readership, your product or service, the occasion, and the person who is signing the letter.

If your prospects don't feel at home with your language, they're not going to buy. Avoid technical words if possible and blown-up language always.

If you're selling apple trees to home growers, be homey. Don't use scientific terms unless they're absolutely necessary. Use a conversational tone, the kind that a farmer (not an agricultural engineer) might use when talking with a neighbor. But stay away from localisms or slang unless you—and your audience—are at home with them.

VIVIDNESS

Colorful language frames whatever you're talking about in a fresh way. Strive for metaphors that *work* extra hard. For instance, in David Ogilvy's classic automobile ad, the ticking clock on the Rolls-Royce dashboard became a metaphor for British engineering skills, style, luxury, and comfort.

Why not make your readers respond with their sensory apparatus, as though they saw the object you're referring to? Actually, you can convey seven different types of sense impressions:

1. Tactile (those you feel)
2. Olfactory (those you smell)
3. Gustatory (those you taste)
4. Visual (those you see)
5. Auditory (those you hear)
6. Motor (those you feel through movement)
7. Kinesthetic (those you feel through muscle sense)

Armed with all these images, you don't have to be content with flat language. You can make your readers active participants in the selling process by asking them to be just a little imaginative. For a book on investing, "the author lights up the dark alleys of commodities trading." For a correspondence course on sailing, you "learn how to read charts with the calm assurance of a steamboat captain steering coolly into the thick fogs of the Mississippi." (Well, perhaps not *that* calmly.)

And Don't Forget . . .

Clarity, appropriateness, and vividness are only three of the basic characteristics of an effective selling style. There are three more points to consider.

1. *A selling style should be quickly understandable.* That doesn't mean you are restricted to using only very simple words. However, you should stick to language your readers are likely to know and use.

2. *A selling style should be more direct and imperative than regular correspondence.* Addressing your prospects directly calls for a heavy use of personal pronouns. Both *you* and *I* should play important roles in your sales material. You have a one-to-one relationship with your reader, which can be very advantageous. Don't walk away from it by being cold and impersonal.

3. *A selling style should contain more restatement than regular correspondence does.* Sometimes in print or broadcast advertising, because of the constraints of design or time, even very important parts of the sales message can be mentioned only once or briefly alluded to and then must be set aside. In a mailing, though, you are in complete control of time and space. Feel free to bring up basic sales points several times if necessary; it can ensure comprehension and a sense of reassurance. But instead of just repeating it, try to restate the point in slightly different language! "Try it for thirty days free." "Live with it for four weeks to see how you like it."

The advantage of an effective style is *control*. You can control all the elements of a sales encounter without being overbearing and still have the prospects respond the way you want.

Why Not Use *Real* Sales Techniques in Copy?

The sound, practical techniques that successful salespeople have long used in personal selling lend themselves very well to direct marketing copy. For instance, good salespeople would hardly start on their rounds without first learning all about the product. How it works. How it's made. How it differs from competing products. Who uses it. Price advantages. Guarantees.

Similarly, by doing your homework, you can make your copy

work harder and sell better. In studying your product, you'll probably come up with more information than you'll ever use. That's fine. It'll prepare you to take advantage of any selling opportunity that comes along, because you will have all the facts at your fingertips. The copywriter who knows the name of General Robert E. Lee's horse can add a very warm and touching note to a package selling a Civil War library. The writer who has bothered to learn how starching restores the appearance of a laundered shirt can sell the services of a pick-up-and-deliver laundry with buttoned-down flair.

Here are some established sales techniques that lend themselves to copy:

• *Sell a deal.* A good salesperson will always have a "special offer"—a quantity discount or a bonus gift—to get one foot in the door. The direct marketing copywriter should work up a good offer, polish the one already in place, or try a variation. For instance, a postscript to your letter offering a cents-off deal for prompt action can speed up orders.

• *Dare to be different.* The salesperson who uses a telegram or fax instead of a phone call to make an appointment gets results. Consider a mailgram (or a fax message) instead of a letter for your next effort.

• *Make the most of your time.* Salespeople who spend too much time on prospects with little potential soon find a lot of time on their hands. Don't waste time writing long letters to people short on interest in what you're selling. Analyze your lists carefully and weed out the poor prospects.

• *Make those calls.* It doesn't do salespeople much good to have a smooth presentation if they don't knock on doors. Don't let too much time go by without having a mailing go out.

• *Stay with your plans.* If salespeople don't stay on their route and work their territory, but instead try to get ahead of the other guy, they'll find ten more salespeople right behind them and five alongside. Copywriters who suddenly get a brainstorm and fly in the face of carefully worked-out strategies and conceptualizations are giving up certain advantages without getting much back in return, except ego satisfaction. Save the inspiration for the next go-around, when it can be carefully analyzed and used properly.

• *Make them think.* An insurance salesman specializing in endowment policies found it tough to convince young prospects of the need for money in their later years. He took a $100 bill, laminated it, and pasted down a border of colored tape. At the end of his presentation, he would pull out this special $100 bill and put it in his prospect's hand, asking, "How many more of these do you want when you are fifty years old?" If you can dramatize a service or concept and leave your prospect thinking, do it. Instead of talking about the rising cost of hospitalization in a supplementary hospital insurance package, enclose facsimiles of actual hospital bills.

• *Let curiosity work for you.* A successful plastics salesperson introduces new samples by carefully wrapping them up in a handsome package and then ignoring the box while he works out the rest of his line with a buyer. Finally, the buyer will ask what's in the box. An envelope legend that piques the reader's curiosity, instead of listing what's inside, can often get the envelope opened more easily.

• *Let the buyer buy.* Don't try to outguess prospects by prejudging their unreadiness to buy. Make a good case for all your wares, selling each product or service enthusiastically and not holding back a particular item "because the market's not yet ready for it." Let the market tell you if it's ready or not.

• *Don't argue.* No salesperson will try to win an argument merely for the sake of winning. That's a good way to lose an order. A commercial promotion that grumbles about politics and taxes or a fund-raising effort that attacks competing charities will just raise hackles while lowering response.

• *Calls are important, but you have to sell too.* Salespeople frequently feel that they have to satisfy their sales manager by making as many calls as possible. A new salesman turned in forty calls for Monday, Tuesday, and Wednesday, but only thirty-nine for Thursday. "What happened?" his sales manager asked. "I was doing okay until the thirty-ninth call. Then he slowed me down by asking me what I was selling." Examine your renewal or collection series, especially the last two or three letters in the series. Are you just going through the motions without making a real effort to sell or persuade?

• *Complainers are good customers.* A salesman knows that the buyer who frequently complains is interested enough to take the time to complain. Save and work that list of complainants. They want attention and they'll often repay your special efforts with a good order. Don't answer a complaint with just a form letter, but attempt to resell and add on.

Good salespeople are persistent and ingenious. Adapt their successful techniques to your next piece of copy and you can find yourself actually selling more because you're selling better.

Use the Order Form to Get More Orders

By the time you get down to writing and designing the order form, you're rather eager to finish off the job and get it into the works. Copy for a direct mail package can sometimes be twenty-five manuscript pages long, involving much time and the work of many people. So the order form sometimes is pushed aside or hurriedly sketched out because it's considered less important than the other components in the package.

A little more time spent in preparing a good order form is worth the extra effort. If the order form can get customers' attention, reinforce their belief in your message, and induce the right sales response, then everything that has preceded it will have done its job. If your order form fails, all your other work will have gone for naught.

What should a good order form consist of? It may pay to prepare a checklist of everything you want the form to do.

☐ *Are all the components in place?* Can the customer identify herself, if personalization or a label is not used? Are any restrictions (deadlines, inducements, legal qualifications) outlined? Have you listed the items for sale and their cost, if you're not using an "open" fill-in form? Have you provided for postage and handling charges, taxes, and methods of payment? Have you made provision for internal handling, including coding and source identification?

☐ *Are all your items in logical sequence?* And are they all necessary? Are you asking for too much information? (A Social Security number on an ad's coupon may discourage orders. You can ask for this information in a followup mailing, after you've heard from the customer.) Have you placed questions in such a way that positive answers will be forthcoming? For instance, ask for a "Yes" answer before a "No" answer when designing check-off boxes.

☐ *Is the design appealing?* Have you allowed enough space for adequate answers? Good typography often goes out the window when order blanks are designed, and the proverbial "fine print" is used instead. Are items well spaced out? Do you shade areas to prevent monotony and emphasize points that should be noted? Do you use a bold typeface to get action?

☐ *Does your language work to get the order?* Are your words communicating clearly? Have you completely and carefully spelled out your warranty to make it explicit, or is your guarantee so hedged with qualifications that it's meaningless? Have you set off salient points with indentations or enumeration?

☐ *Is the order form useful to the customer?* Is it easy to use? Will using it make customers feel that they'll get the product or service sooner and without any trouble? Or does it resemble a legal contract? Does the order form make an attempt to sell? Or does it "instruct" the customers with negatives, regulations, and commands? The order form should not "order" customers; it should convince them to buy.

☐ *Is the order form flattering?* All too often, order forms have been designed solely for internal use rather than customer convenience. Are items addressed to the customer's needs or experience? Or are they too abstract and pedantic? Or simplistic and childish? A legalistic contract may discourage a warehouse supervisor looking for a good, cheap source of cartons.

☐ *Is the order form adequate for your fulfillment needs?* It's not good to have a well-designed, well-written order form that only impedes order processing. Is there room for computation by your fulfillment people, if need be? Are all codes and prices listed? Does the order form allow the company to gather information and supply goods and services without any trouble? If possible, get the final user—the fulfillment department, mail room, or service bureau— to look over your order form. And test several different order forms for format, comprehensibility, and flow of information.

A little extra care in preparing the order form or coupon can pay off in orders that might otherwise be lost because of misunderstanding, resentment, or impatience.

The Opacity Measure:
How Dense Is Your Message?

Teachers of reading measure the comprehensibility of a given piece of text with various standards. Applying an assortment of values, these measurements may show, for instance, that a particular essay, story, or book is too difficult for a certain level of reading achievement.

Direct mail also has a benchmark of comprehensibility—*rate of response*—although it is usually referred to as a measure of success or failure rather than understandability.

The reason for this is simple. We usually toss a direct mail package into battle with the assumption that its message, offer, and appeal are all clear and understandable. Everybody concerned with the message may agree what it should say, but sometimes too much is assumed, and we don't pay sufficient attention to the logical threads holding the story together.

It might be a technical matter that is inadvertently glossed over. Or a step in the sales argument that isn't carefully explained. Or some term that isn't clearly defined. (When something is defined, the explanation should aid the sales pitch, rather than just provide a piece of passive information. *Example:* "Imagine this Blue Willow pattern occupying pride of place in your collection as it winsomely captures all the charm of ancient China" rather than a perfunctory "The Blue Willow design is often found on household china.")

If the rate of response does double duty as an index of comprehensibility, or opacity measure, you'll find it becomes twice as valuable. Here's why: If you mail to two lists that seem similar and the response rate is far apart, your first instinct is to say that the poorly performing list just wasn't right for the offer. But it's also possible that those on the poorly performing list didn't understand the message. Not only because the language was too opaque or just plain wrong for the audience, but maybe the very thrust of the package was incorrectly targeted.

Some obvious examples: Building contractors specializing in hospitals may not understand a lavish package promoting the esthetic advantages of "period" hardware, a package eagerly responded to by home builders. A cookbook on East Indian cuisine may leave mail order wok buyers cold. Dog groomers may not understand the need for a gadget that veterinarians drool over. Human resource managers may not see why they should own a software program that employee benefits managers swear by.

But what if the differences in lists aren't that obvious? What if you're getting strangely disparate responses from apparently similar lists, such as upscale catalog buyers, or investors, or subscribers?

If your response rates show that certain lists are clustered together in an inexplicable pattern—response rates of 0.5, 1.25, and 1.48 percent from lists that seem to have the same parameters as your control list, which is delivering 2.50 percent—it can mean that the message that is being read loud and clear by the control audience is being blurred for other lists.

What to do? Have the package picked apart in a survey of sample members of the strangely performing audiences.

You may discover that you're using regionalisms that have little meaning to them but were responded to favorably by the control list. Or you may have gotten a list of prospects who just didn't understand the message. Another obvious example: Both pharmacists (whose training is scientific and technical) and grocers (with a background in marketing and buying) are retailers, but would grocers understand—or *want* to understand—a technical pitch for a one-hour photo-developing mini-lab, a pitch that may have worked well for the original camera store control list?

So, in addition to other standards—graphic appeal, offer, seasonability—why not apply the opacity measure, the criterion of comprehension? It may help clear up the reasons for an otherwise inexplicable response.

It Pays to Be "Forgetful" in Direct Marketing Copy

Some of the most successful practitioners of direct response are the most forgetful people in business. Well, not really forgetful, because they've remembered that human curiosity can often overcome sales resistance.

Consider all the mailings you've received that included a very long letter. Yet, at the end of the four-page or even eight-page letter, you'll find that the writer "forgot" to tell you something and had to include a P.S. Forgot? No. The writer remembered a basic rule of direct mail: *The postscript is always read.* And it should be composed as carefully as your opening paragraph. Trouble is, a lot of copywriters are awfully tired by the time it comes to signing the letter and they forget to use the P.S. as the powerful tool it can be. Use the P.S. to ram a message home, to prompt the prospect to return the order card, or to repeat the free offer. Don't let it go to waste. And consider using simulated handwriting instead of the same typeface you've used for the body of the letter.

The "publisher's letter" or "lift letter" is another example of thoughtful forgetfulness. Instead of having the sales manager fret about the prospect missing the wonderful opportunity, why not have the original letter writer scrawl a hurried memo, perhaps on her own memo paper? "Hurry, the offer must expire soon!" or "Nearly forgot . . . you have only fifteen more days to answer, then the books must be closed forever!"

Another "last-minute" device is to have the writer scrawl the note on a business card in red ink or pencil. Fund raisers often use pencil-scrawled notes from real people to push home their particular message. While not really last-minute notes, these intensely personal messages add a dramatic urgency.

Using a different-colored ink in the body of a letter also conveys a sense of personal urgency. Publishers Clearing House decorates its letters with marginalia, annotations, circled paragraphs, and underscored sentences. There's a rushed, last-minute feeling that isn't at all subtle—and is very effective. Your order card, too, need not be a pristine piece of printing. Help the prospect fill out the form by noting special terms, a sales price, or a deadline. Publishers Clearing House "okays credit" with a handwritten message.

As a kid, you may have sent or received letters that had cryptic messages on the envelope—code words, initials, whatever. Use this idea and "handwrite" a message on the outer envelope. This last-minute, just-before-you-dropped-it-in-the-mailbox ploy can be more effective to the right market than a handsomely typeset teaser. And instead of an expensively printed brochure, consider a number of loose photographs with messages written on them in white ink. This device is especially appropriate when you're selling travel and tourism.

Another warmly personal and "written-in-haste" device is the followup postcard. If you are selling a subscription to a travel magazine, or a tour package, or a sweepstakes offering a vacation prize, follow up the original mailing with a "written" picture postcard: "Wish you were here! You can be, when you subscribe to *Sybarite Monthly*, only $15 for two months. Just call me today!"

This handwritten, last-minute comment can also be used to good effect on catalogs, where you can scrawl pertinent notes throughout, almost like a catalog shopper making notes. Things like "Only 150 of these left" or "We made a special deal on these" or "Don't forget to order one of these" can be a friendly postscript when not overdone.

There are a few rules for the effective use of handwritten postscripts:

1. Repeat a point only if it is worth repeating.
2. Use simple words and phrases whose meanings are unmistakably clear.
3. Use enthusiastic words. Convey urgency and excitement.
4. Be friendly.
5. Don't be smart or clever. Nobody will understand you.
6. Don't be subtle. You can use powerhouse tactics here, including lots of underscoring, exclamation marks, and asterisks.

Try to remember to drop in a last-minute note or urgent P.S. That's using direct mail as the immediate, personal, memorable medium it was intended to be.

Winning Strategies for Managing Consumers, Competition, and Markets

Don't Sell Yourself Short: Ask for More Than Your Share

As any salesperson can tell you, the fastest way to boost your income is to increase the size of each sale you make. However, direct marketers often refuse to be creative in this area. They insist on asking for a standard-size order, even though the prospect may want to order something larger. This rigidness may come from distaste for the inordinate amount of paperwork needed to change a standard order, or it may go back to a certain timidity about rocking the boat. But if you make an effort to get a sale, why not raise your sights? Here are some ideas you may want to consider.

1. Think in terms of getting an order that's two, three, even six times larger than standard. How? By reselling prospects while they're still enthusiastic about their initial purchase. When prospects become subscribers and say, "I'll take six months of your magazine," offer them the opportunity to extend their subscription to a year, even two.

You can strike while the iron is cooling off, by offering them a chance to renew long before the current subscription expires. Consider them your friends (they haven't canceled, have they?) so they may be very receptive to the early-bird opportunity to renew and save money.

2. Spend less time with small fry. If you spend two-thirds of your effort on little fellows who give you only one-third of your volume, you're dying by thirds. There's no need to drop the small customer entirely, but spend less money on catalogs and expensive mailings. Use the phone or send a form letter once a quarter with an inexpensive circular. By concentrating your efforts where they can bring in the most profitable orders, you'll harvest more with less trouble.

Try to sell "big." Instead of a discount, weigh the possibility of a deluxe offer. If you're selling a book, use your order form to tout a leather binding with gold letters. If your prospect is looking at the order form, you've just about sold him anyway. At this stage, you won't alienate him by offering a deluxe version.

Experiment with a Ferrari-type list. C.O.M.B. Direct Marketing Corp. of Minneapolis, a leading liquidator and distress-merchandise vendor, regularly advertises its terrific buys in *The Wall Street Journal*.

3. Move your borderline customers to a new frontier. In other words, use ideas to move your customers up to higher-priced products. One surefire idea is the "write your own ticket" offer. Magazines have been using this for some time: instead of nineteen weeks for $17.00, let subscribers choose the number of weeks they'd like at $0.89 an issue.

4. Spark more sales with this step-up transformer: When an order comes in, do more than merely acknowledge or fill it—promote an additional product. This can be done with a sales message on the shipping form or on the invoice. If you're selling business to business, where parcels are opened up by people who aren't making buying decisions, send a copy of the shipping form to the original purchaser.

5. Are you sure your customer only wants one item? If a customer orders one book, dare to sell him two. Mention the second book on that order form (it's getting crowded, isn't it?). If he's bought hunting boots, sell him shoelaces and waterproofing.

6. Don't hold your customer back. (Yes, customers often think bigger than suppliers.) Always ask for more than a minimum order. Be careful, though, about confusing your customers. Don't turn a simple ad into a catalog offering many products. You can give them the opportunity to trade up, but don't give them the chance to throw their hands up in total confusion.

There are still other offers you can use, including the multiproduct "piggyback" offer that features one product in an ad, with complementary items as an afterthought; and the famous "good, better, best" offer that goes the deluxe offer one better by offering the customer three choices instead of one or two!

Get More Mileage From Your Mailing List

A company's mailing list represents one of its strongest assets. It is not only a selling tool, but also a gauge of the strengths and weaknesses of the business. It's also a barometer of marketing trends that can help provide solutions to selling problems.

When a mailing list is studied carefully, there are eight situations—at least—in which a targeted mailing can give a significant boost to an organization.

1. *Quashing local competition.* What should you do if a branch of another bank opens in a neighborhood you've long considered "safe," or another supermarket opens across the street?

Instead of costly shotgun mass print and broadcasting advertising, a threatened retail operation can often counter with targeted mailings that make a series of special offers to current customers. A distributor or supplier who finds a competitor camped in his backyard could go on the offensive by mailing a special offer to selected retailers. The quantity and quality of data that theoretically you alone have access to can make the difference in putting out brushfires of this nature. Personalized mailings can make an appeal that no competitor can equal.

2. *Using time to your advantage.* Have you been watching the seasonality of purchases? In addition to Christmas or vacation buying, your customers may be marching to the beats of some other drummers: the start of the school year, or April 15. Seasonal mailings to exploit these purchasing rhythms can bring a new cycle of profits to the alert mailer.

3. *Digging more gold from a rich mine.* A book club may have a number of members who take only the most expensive offerings. Using a lifestyle locator overlay (a segmenting tool that matches lifestyle characteristics with buyers), a catalog house may find that a good proportion of its customers are heavy potential purchasers. Or the old "80/20" rule may hold true: an employment agency discovers that 20 percent of its clients account for 80 percent of its business. Massage the names that have higher than usual purchasing potential through additional and intensive mailings, perhaps isolating them and giving them a special identity ("carriage trade" or "VIP" customers).

4. *Buttressing sagging segments.* Looking through your sales reports, do you see one territory lagging behind the others? Or is one SIC (Standard Industrial Classification) falling behind? This may need a two-pronged effort, involving both direct mailing and telemarketing. If your mailing list includes telephone numbers, you can reinforce a mailing with a personal call to those slow buyers.

5. *Celebrating or cleaning.* What should you do about those customers who haven't bought anything in a year? Make a special occasion of it! On the anniversary of the purchase, mail a reminder to the customer, and include a special offer. If you don't hear from him, chop him.

6. *Rewarding.* You may want to share the benefits of a lucky purchase with some of your best customers—especially if inventory is too light to warrant a mailing to your entire list. An occasional goodwill gesture to your best customers can pay dividends. It can also move some merchandise that is taking up too much space.

7. *Renew friendships.* Some customers start out like a house afire, buying heavily and often. Then their "RFM" (recency/frequency/dollar amount of purchase) begins to slacken. If this isn't an overall pattern that can be traced to economic or industry conditions or some problem in your company, it may call for some personal hand holding. A customer's enthusiasm for a firm—whether it's a bank, a clothing store, or a charitable organization—can wane when the only contact is an impersonal catalog or a statement stuffer. Then it's time for the manager or president to send a letter on personal stationery to keep the customer from straying. A simple reference to the date of the last purchase, donation, or visit can tell customers that you care about them and that they're not a faceless number.

8. *Making room and profits.* End-of-season sales and inventory clearances are popular revenue producers. While many customers will respond to them, a check of your mailing list may show that certain customers buy *only* at these times. You may want to do a special limited mailing to these discount customers, perhaps clearing out merchandise without "cheapening" your line with your entire list.

In addition to any regular program of mailings you may be doing, consider frequent mailings to chosen segments of your list. It can revitalize names and bring in new profits.

Selling Against the Grain: The Perilous (but Profitable) Art of Contrarian Direct Marketing

Conventional wisdom dictates that, to be effective, direct marketing must be carefully aimed at the proper audience. All well and good, but very often objectivity flies out the window when the final list of lists is being drawn up and the test assault is being readied.

Has this ever happened to you on the eve of a mailing? Somebody gets nervous and orders several more lists, very similar to those already chosen. This sort of suspenders-and-belt reinforcement can muddy the waters. Irrelevant factors come into play, and a list package on which you have worked to eliminate as many variables as possible suddenly plays host to conditionals that throw everything askew: price consideration instead of product choice, well-aged frequent purchasers versus hotline names, or subscribers versus lifestyles.

Yet there are times when it pays to make an otherwise simple test structure more complex. For instance, a mailer might want to see if there is a target audience that has never been reached because of outdated assumptions or a mailing pattern inherited from previous management. Take the case of three specialized book clubs faced with a problem in common: declining results.

The first—originally designed as a family do-it-yourself club— tries to jolt sales with "a better offer": more free books and a looser commitment ("Take six books for only $1 and buy only two more."). The mailing goes to the same audience as always. Results are fine, according to the low standards the book club has set for itself, but quality falls off later in the membership cycle.

The second book club, for hobbyists, decides that the fault is in the mix of books. So it offers, in addition to its line of specialized books, a range of more popular books, posters, and even office supplies—thus blurring its image and thoroughly confusing its target market.

Book club no. 3, a business executives' book club, believes its problem may be a change of audience. There is evidence that its old audience may not be replenishing itself as in the past. New patterns are arising. Skills are no longer easy to learn by simply cracking books. Seminars are growing in popularity. And people entering the business world have a different orientation toward self-improvement. So, in addition to traditional lists, several mailings are reserved for lists that are very different. For instance, a mailing is made overseas to Pacific Basin businesspeople. Another mailing is made stateside to Korean and East Indian entrepreneurs. And a third one goes not to established businesspeople, but to middle managers who may have taken early retirement and are now looking for new horizons to conquer.

When the results are studied, it becomes evident that several new markets have developed for the same old books: overseas business-people, newcomers to the American business scene, and would-be business owners (all markets that would never have been thoroughly exploited with the old mailing patterns).

Perhaps these truths would have been seen with careful preanaly-sis and a little hypothesizing, but direct mail's emphasis on taking careful aim on a target sometimes puts blinders on a marketer who ignores peripheral possibilities.

When does it pay to be contrary in picking lists for a direct mail test? One or more of these conditions should be present:

1. *Loss of market share.* Perhaps the audience is still there—but under a different name.
2. *Gradual deterioration of results.* Sometimes in an older com-pany, habits linger on, and tired mailing programs that worked a decade ago are still being used.
3. *Acceptance of flawed judgment.* This takes tremendous cour-age on the part of a mailer—to admit he or she may be wrong even before the exercise begins. Especially with a brand-new product, concept, or company, the givens may not really be what they seem. You wouldn't send an expensive encyclope-dia offering to addresses on Hard Scrabble Road, would you? Well, why not . . . if you can come up with an easy payment plan, and you can promise with a fair degree of certainty that the customers or their children might eventually move from Hard Scrabble Road across the tracks to Easy Street, thanks to the knowledge and wisdom found in the encyclopedia.
4. *Potential for rollout.* One of the many disappointments in

direct mail is the list that does well in a test but is too small for a real rollout.

At the experimental stage, if you have the budget to add a contrary list to the mix, make sure it's not in there just for the sake of contrariness. It should be able to support itself if it does work (recognizing that the odds against its doing well are extremely high). It should teach you something about the nature of the offer, price, product, and market. (Perhaps you need to go back and review the entire project.) It should not detract from the main thrust of the mailing by robbing money from the budget. And going against the grain shouldn't be interpreted as a license to abandon prudence and judgment. For instance, don't consider obviously undesirable lists. (In the heady early days of credit-card solicitations, mass mailings that eventually cost the sponsors huge sums in uncollectable debts were made without simple credit checks.)

By being careful and selective, the direct marketer may be able to take advantage of the strengths and hidden advantages in contrary lists. Even if a list is not actually used, the exercise of considering the unconsidered can stretch the marketing mind.

The Name Game: Opportunities in Creative Demographics

As if we hadn't had enough segmentation from sociodemographics, along comes CACI, the database people responsible for ACORN (A Classification of Residential Neighborhoods), to announce still another weapon in the never-ending fight against anonymity: "Monica," or the name-game plan.

According to the British publication *Marketing Week*, CACI in England has computerized every first name in Great Britain to develop name clusters that give away one's age. The theory is that there are trends in naming children.

For instance, in the United States, "Franklin" probably belongs to a man born between 1933 and 1945, the years Franklin Delano Roosevelt was president. Shirley was a popular first name during the

Depression, when the child movie star Shirley Temple ruled the box office. When Grace Kelly became Princess of Monaco, thousands of girls received her name.

Every year, someone dutifully reports the most popular first name of the past twelve months, and every year newspapers dutifully print this information, sometimes alongside the list of the ten most popular dog breeds or song hits or movies.

CACI wields this information to drop an overlay on a mailing list and spot ages. So a mail order insurance company looking for men born after 1939 but before 1960 can write to all the Dwights (for Dwight D. Eisenhower) and Douglases (for Douglas MacArthur) and be reasonably sure that they are not writing either to centenarians or to first-graders.

While some names like John or Mary resist fashion, there seem to be enough valid patterns to give mass mailers still another tool with which to segment their audiences.

Of course a creative mailer needn't stop at name clusters. There are imaginative variations on this idea. So a computer company trying to sell its machines to the class of 1991 addresses not only their parents but also alumni of the classes of the 1960s—college graduates and possible parents who may have escaped the list compilers' sifting. A copywriter raising funds for a far-off mission not only uses a denominational appeal but also casts a nonsectarian net to pull in travelers and tourists to the region under consideration. A smoke detector company not only mails to homeowners but to mortgage lenders who have more than a passing interest in keeping property intact and who may influence or endorse a purchase. And while residents of retirement communities aren't ready to buy tricycles or roller skates for themselves, they are interested in equipping their grandchildren with appropriate transportation.

There's nothing solid about the marketplace. It keeps shifting. New allegiances and new identities consistently crop up. It is therefore the task of the direct marketer to take advantage of possible affinities and interests that aren't apparent at first glance. The segmentation of a population by first names or age clusters is a good example of this kind of creative vision, remolding information into a key that unlocks new opportunities.

Outflanking the Competition

What happens when a book-club concept, mail order item, or some other product or service matures? When the saturation point has been reached and most potential buyers have bought what you're selling, while sales and profits drop and competition intensifies?

The odds are good that the only way to get more business is to lure it away from the present competition; in this late state of the marketing cycle, not many new competitors are apt to enter the arena. The goal now is to increase market share, not sales. And one way to get a larger share of the market is to remold the product or service so that the consumer perceives it differently.

Changing the image of a product or service may call for any or all of these three management tactics:

1. Thinking of major modifications, improvements, or innovations
2. Coming up with new uses for the service or product
3. Beating the bushes for new users

There is also a fourth method. It demands ingenuity and direct marketing skill, but it can be quite cost-effective. This is the so-called flanker product or service, brought on stage for one purpose: to support the sales of the main product. Because it bears the same name as the main item, it benefits from all the previous advertising and from transferred customer loyalty (the famous "halo effect").

The flanker item may be an accessory. For instance, if you're selling desk diaries and calendars by mail to businesspeople and professionals, you may offer a line of pocket diaries, thus expanding the concept of diary keeping.

Book clubs may branch out into newsletters. A specialized book club offering books on pediatric nursing may publish a newsletter with excerpts from these books plus more timely news and information. Most book clubs already issue a reader's report to whet members' appetites for upcoming selections. With very little effort, this utilitarian—and free—publication can be turned into a valuable revenue generator. Or a magazine may start up a book club as an adjunct to its publishing efforts, offering substantial discounts to readers of specialized remaindered or closed-out titles.

Several years ago, a seminar production company began taping the events it sponsored and sold edited cassettes to people who couldn't be there in person. It then transcribed the proceedings and sold the printed versions to people who wanted permanent reference tools. The next step? Perhaps to close the loop by publishing abridgements of the books in a regularly issued newsletter, as a giveaway promotion.

Flanker products or services can spark sales of the much more profitable "parent" item: Mail order shoe companies can sell shoe trees, travel agencies can offer passport wallets, and mail order gourmet food suppliers might publish cookbooks.

Testing various ideas and then carefully analyzing results will help the direct marketer find the most effective "flanker" and use it to boost sales of the mature service or product. So, before withdrawing from the marketplace, give that tried-and-true item a second chance with a flanker, and go around the competition.

Selling to People Who Influence Others

In the 1950s, a promotion campaign for a woman's service magazine urged advertisers to "reach the influentials"—the magazine's readers, who were presumably in a position to influence others.

Sociologists have long been aware of the impact of influence on buyer behavior. "Reference-group" theory, for instance, postulates that a buyer's attitudes, opinions, and values are influenced by a group of people whose standards serve as frames of reference. A homeowner's neighborhood, a worker's office, a parishioner's church, a shortstop's team—they all set norms for the behavior of members. It was also felt that there was a seepage of influence downward to outsiders who might never have any contact with influencers. Occasionally, a vestige of this old "snob appeal" belief surfaces, as with the "old money" advertising for Ralph Lauren fashions.

However, researchers as long ago as 1955 (Katz and Lazarsfeld,

Personal Influence) saw that opinion leadership was actually a horizontal phenomenon for many products and ideas, with the influencer dealing directly with peers.

KEY-PERSON STRATEGY

One result of these "horizontal information flow" studies was the adoption of the *key-person marketing strategy*, which says that there are really two key people in a group: the innovator (first to buy) and the influential (the tastemaker). Move them, and you've moved the group.

Direct marketers can benefit from this technique. If you can identify the key people in a group and persuade them to buy your service or product, you'll find other group members following the leader.

Examples: The computer manufacturer who targets "the best and the brightest" students in a class and offers them discounts; the car importer who goes after the owner of the biggest house in an upscale neighborhood; and the fund raiser who tries to interest senior corporate management in supporting her cause.

INNOVATORS AND INFLUENTIALS

How does a direct marketer identify members of these groups? While labels have a way of changing, we can define innovators as usually being the first to adopt something new. Venturesome and daring, they may have a higher social status than other members of the group. More money and relative youth are also criteria.

On the other hand, the influentials are *tastemakers* who, while respected opinion leaders, are not too different from others in their group. They'll have local rather than cosmopolitan interests (fewer trips to Europe, perhaps, or fewer mail order purchases of exotic foods). More deliberate than the innovators, they won't be first to try something new, but they will be early. Perhaps because of this more mature and deliberate behavior, others in their peer group respect their taste.

CHANGING IDENTITIES

If you're looking for a list of innovators and influentials, try subscribers to upscale publications and members of specialized book clubs. Both innovators and influentials are known frequenters of impersonal, objective sources of information, rather than being dependent on word of mouth.

But remember that innovators and influentials also have the bothersome habit of changing identities. It's important to realize that an influential person in group A may be a skeptic or deliberate buyer or even a "laggard" in group B, especially when the buying decision has to do with professional and business matters.

Businesslike Ways of Selling to Business

When you are setting up a direct marketing program for business, it's helpful to look at the sort of purchaser and the type of purchase called for. There are usually three types of purchases that you would ask a commercial or institutional end user to make: a frequent repeat purchase, an infrequent repeat purchase, and a one-time purchase.

If you're asking for a frequent repeat purchase from an institutional end user, your approach will be different from the one you use to sell a project to an original equipment manufacturer. Basically, you have to provide for significant differences in needs and wants, and especially in benefits and advantages.

COMMERCIAL END USERS

A commercial end user making a *frequent repeat purchase* is probably buying supplies or replacement parts, for something like a soap factory or printing company. If there is a specialized sales force in place serving these end users, your direct marketing would be devised to support the field people. Or there may be independent distributors and dealers who could benefit from your promotion.

Several important decisions are called for, based on your requirements for effective coverage and impact. For instance, if you run a couponed ad in trade papers with direct mail support, should the rest of your dollars be spent at conventions and on premiums?

Other commercial end users, such as office or restaurant equipment manufacturers, may purchase equipment on an *infrequent repeat purchase* basis. To reach them, you may use your direct sales force, a manufacturers' representative, or a distributor. Here your promotion not only sells the end user, but also establishes and maintains a mutually profitable relationship with your agents, distributors, and dealers.

You may want to do a mailing to your contact personnel that keeps them up-to-date on your promotions to your customers, encouraging them to operate closely with your organization. This kind of promotion to agents, distributors, and dealers is of utmost significance, since it establishes close contact, develops a good reputation, and builds a friendly long-range relationship with organizations that can sustain your company for years to come.

How do you promote the *one-time purchase*, say major equipment for the operation of a facility? How do you sell air conditioning to a hotel or an important testing device to hospital equipment manufacturers? Through your direct sales force, a contractor, or a manufacturers' agent.

In this case, it's important to enhance exposure for prospecting, preselling, and actual selling. An education program to facilitate customer use, plus application and other technical assistance, is also called for. You may want to consider an educational "curriculum" mailing, a series of mailings in the form of newsletters or informative brochures.

How do you establish yourself as a source of periodic or continuous supply of products for resale to commercial users (perhaps food companies or camera manufacturers)? Through a direct sales force, agent, or distributor.

You have to build friendly relationships with buyers, prospects, and sellers. This is often done with trade advertising, sales promotion, publicity, and identification programs to build product acceptance.

INDUSTRIAL END USERS

What if you're selling supplies or replacement parts to an industrial end user such as a lubricant producer? This *frequent repeat purchase* can be sold through a direct sales force, distributor, jobber, or agent; support them with a steady communications flow about your product, service, and value to customers.

While this usually takes the form of updated production specification sheets, you may steal a march on competitors by building a promotion that your customer looks forward to: an ongoing contest, premiums for purchases (small TV sets, for instance; hospital and health-care equipment manufacturers have been known to offer similar premiums through direct mail), or a discount plan that competitors could have offered but didn't.

Infrequent repeat purchases of industrial equipment by industrial end users may be made through your own sales force, distributors, agents, or contractors. As an example, testing-equipment manufacturers have infrequent need for certain parts that become obsolete or worn. How do you sell to them? Through a creative and systematic persuasion method that takes into account how and where your customers want to be helped.

This calls for research—getting people into the field to meet with your customers and reviewing their needs and concerns. You'll learn which media work best, whether you ought to install audio-visual selling techniques such as video cassettes or training seminars, or whether your purchasing decision makers react best to direct mail or couponed ads.

What if you're selling a massive component to a machine-tool manufacturer? This *one-time purchase* of major plant equipment may be handled directly or through a contractor.

Contractors play an important role. But have you been neglecting your contractors in favor of your own direct selling force? Perhaps you need to do an analysis of your contractors' selling needs or a market development program for enlarging the market.

Perhaps you should put into place a third-party direct marketing program, issued by contractors but created by your firm.

If you're selling material on a frequent repeat-purchase plan for use in a consumer product—for instance, a dye in foodstuffs—your direct selling force or manufacturers' agents need support through a reminder direct marketing program that keeps your name up front. Gimmicks, contests, and premiums come into their own here, but it is also important to prospect, presell, and sell as well as entertain.

GOVERNMENT PROJECTS

Direct marketing can serve a purpose when one sells contracts and projects to the government. Whether the selling is through direct sales or through a government contractor, innovative advertising and public relations can build company and product acceptance. In-house publishing can create an image for your organization, preempting a competitor's efforts. For example, a free subscription series of booklets or monographs can establish your organization's credentials in technical areas.

Studying the customer's needs and building a direct marketing effort that will offer various benefits and advantages calls for a program of analytical study. This analysis should include customer classification, type of purchases, nature of product, and distribution channel employed. Once this analysis is in place, a direct marketing approach appropriate for each specific situation can be selected, tailored to the specific needs of the marketplace.

Can Direct Marketing and Retailing Coexist?

A company selling to the public through retailers *and* direct marketing can encounter serious conflicts. For instance, it isn't rare for retailers, whether franchised dealers or stores carrying the company's line, to complain that a company's direct marketing efforts (catalogs, direct mail, or mail order print and broadcast advertising) compete for the same finite customer base. On the other hand, direct marketers are sometimes apt to dismiss retailers as sleepy order takers at best or promotion-crazed price slashers at worst.

Can these two groups ever work out their differences? Perhaps there is a way for their antagonism to be muted; there may even be a way for both functions—retailing and direct marketing—to be simultaneously strengthened while coexisting.

Making War

It might pay to examine the most prominent points of contention, those areas where retailer and direct marketer repeatedly bump heads.

PROMOTION AND ADVERTISING

Imagine having a publisher's mail order book promotion (complete with early-bird discount) land in every reader's mailbox in an author's hometown just as the local bookstore has put the final touches on an elaborate and costly autograph party. Or listen to the sales department's tirade when a local retailer demands co-op advertising dollars for an ad featuring a top-of-the-line product as a loss leader.

Promotion and advertising problems can be worsened by the divergent needs of the company and the retailer. A manufacturer seeks to create consumer demand directly *or* indirectly; the retailer wants customer traffic—directly.

PRICING STRUCTURE AND SPECIAL OFFERS

Cents-off promotion, sampling, and discount offers can help promote a product and drive customers into the stores. But when the same offers are made to customers through a direct mail campaign that totally ignores the retailer, with responses going back to the company, this can wipe out years of patient missionary work on the part of the sales staff—something that still happens in book publishing.

Publishing offers another special problem: book clubs. A title that sells for $17.95 through stores may be offered for only $11.00 or even $1.00 by a book club. The argument that book-club promotions tend to send nonclub readers into bookshops won't convince retailers who see their market for a popular title vanish because of book-club offers. And if the book club is one that happens to be run by the publisher, the problem is exacerbated.

On the other hand, retailers who heavily discount a product—perhaps by picking up distress merchandise at bankruptcy auctions, through international gray markets, or by dumping old inventory—can be intensely painful to manufacturers.

DELIVERY AND DISTRIBUTION, SCHEDULING, AND FORECASTING

Manufacturers who sell directly to the public and offer free delivery for cash with order may be causing trouble for local retailers who pass along delivery charges. Manufacturers who promise prompt delivery to consumers while not filling special single-item orders for retailers, or drop ship a product without using the retailer's carefully prepared shipping label, guarantee a rather hot reception for their salespeople the next time they venture into retail-land.

And the poor salesperson who writes up a book full of advance orders, only to have them canceled at the assembly line, won't be terribly willing to go out on a limb and forecast his territory's needs. (Can you predict a product's success or failure with a direct mail test? If it's going to be sold in stores, you may want to enlist the retailer's support with a parallel promotion.)

Direct mail can come to the aid of manufacturers dealing with retailers who habitually over-order on consignment and then blithely send back their returns while the warehouse is clogged. Here direct marketers can consult their records and extrapolate possible sales for like products, guiding both overambitious sales-people and eternally hopeful retailers.

Some other areas where direct marketing and retailing compete, rather than cooperate, are new-product introduction and support services (repair and installation). The problem of other links in the distribution channel, such as wholesalers and brokers whose opera-tions may be independent of both manufacturer and retailer, gives rise to another basis for conflict.

So we have two sets of criteria. On the one hand, direct marketers working for a company are eager to expand sales, build brand loyalty, achieve multiple distribution, and enter new markets. Retailers, who want store sales, customer loyalty, exclusivity, pro-motion, and display of profitable items, see the activities of a direct marketing unit as a declaration of war. Yet to the direct marketer, a retailer's perceived inefficiencies are harming his company and its products.

Making Peace

Perhaps the answer is to take advantage of each function's capabili-ties. Retailers can reach a given location again and again. Direct marketing can target a market, sell on a one-to-one basis, and elicit a keyed response.

Direct marketers might want to design programs that bring retailers into the operation. Send mail out under the letterhead of local retailers or direct the customers to local, listed stores. Prepare ad "slicks" and packaged campaigns for retailers to use. Or go after business that retailers are usually not prepared to handle—government or institutional sales.

If company policy dictates that direct marketing exist as a competitor or alternative to retailers, then treat direct marketing as a retailer—with the same range of discounts, with the same provision for delivery and special offers. The direct marketing unit then could become the "national retailer" for the brand, perhaps making the product available where no shop exists. To keep peace in the family, an anonymous name could be chosen for the direct marketing arm of a company, with a different address as well. Perhaps a separate model of the product could be created for direct marketing purposes, with just a cosmetic change or label change. Before you set up this sort of operation, have your lawyers investigate possible problems with the Robinson-Patman Act of 1936 and the FTC rulings.

Direct marketers may want to spend time in the field, working in retail outlets to analyze both customers and storekeepers, so that the needs of both are understood. And retailers may use the skills of the direct marketing unit in promoting more effectively to their marketing area.

Stress and strife between direct marketers and retailers can be lessened through increased cooperation, which will benefit not only both functions but also the customer.

Five Keys to Direct Marketing Growth

Success in direct marketing is too often measured solely by the results of the latest mailing. However, to sustain success, a direct marketing company has to look on itself as something more than a mailing machine, and prepare for those times when a mailing lays an egg, the economy turns sour, or the competition steals a march.

Direct marketers can benefit by using the five strategies common to most successful businesses.

1. *Set growth goals.* A corporate growth philosophy sets a goal that every department can contribute to. This could be a simply worded but very ambitious mandate such as: "Grow faster than the economy." Or it can use an internal measure, with management decreeing that sales and profits double in the next five years. The important thing is an articulated goal to which all employees can dedicate their efforts.

2. *Know when to change strategy.* The catalog operator who knows how to interpret seemingly insignificant blips and makes plans to drop a marginal department, the book club that reads buying patterns and increases promotions of different subjects, the mail order company that understands the concept of product life cycles and unemotionally discards a traditional item—these are the firms that remain in phase with developmental patterns. Every industry encounters change. For some, it is quite slow; for others, it can be a roller coaster ride. To acknowledge the possibility of change, and to have a plan in place, are signs of a level-headed company that can weather most storms.

3. *Move into new areas before competition does.* Direct marketers have at their command one of the most potent marketing tools known: the order file. You can quickly learn to sense changes in buying patterns, and you can test your impressions very economically. Is a new piece of electronic gear selling well because of powerful copy on that particular item, or are customers actually more receptive to new technology? Why are certain zip codes bringing in more than their usual share of new names? By systematically testing any new marketing possibility, you can have a plan of action in place when growth rate begins to fall off and it's time to move on to new products and new markets.

4. *Test new fields before entering them.* By evaluating possible opportunities, especially their vitality and staying power, a direct marketing company can avoid problems later on. So instead of a catalog house investing millions in a new leisurewear catalog, it can test the waters with a few pages in its current catalog, statement stuffers, or inexpensive letters. Then, the company can examine the body of evidence thus amassed and make decisions based on fact, not hunch.

5. *Drop losing products.* Older companies may suffer from a conspiracy of sentiment. The original concept that worked so well for the Founding Father is sometimes carried on for several generations, even though it's a drag on profits and morale. It's only when a new owner comes in or a brash new generation throws open the windows that everybody suddenly realizes what an albatross some of the old products were.

To keep an objective viewpoint, some catalog companies demand that each item in their book produce a certain amount of income. All well and good, but a minimum expectation has a way of being lowered for favorites. So the resources and skills of a profitable magazine are unfairly diverted to a prestigious book division and the abilities of a vitamin distributor are wasted hawking last year's health fad.

Rare is the flexible company with a firm growth plan in place that can take advantage of opportunities without jumping at every novelty. But direct marketing offers marketing analysis and testing tools that allow a company with a sure sense of its identity to move in new directions productively.

CHAPTER 3

Smart Tactics to Maintain Your Edge

Know Your Product

Before you can create an effective promotion, you should have an accurate picture of the product or service you're selling. This detailed analysis will give you the ammunition you need to sell skillfully. Even if you don't use every fact that you've unearthed, you'll have the confidence to move details around, omit unnecessary facts, and emphasize significant ones.

The best way to build this analysis is in five steps.

STEP 1. DETERMINE THE CHARACTERISTICS OF WHAT YOU'RE SELLING

Look into concrete things, such as the way the product is made or how the company is organized. Acquire as much paper as

68

possible: descriptions, press releases, ads, and brochures. Talk to the public relations department. Check with industry and government organizations. Read the company's annual report. Read magazine articles about the product or service. Don't skip the fine print; footnotes, charts and obscure tables may be dull, but to the researcher they're often gold.

For instance, a copywriter assigned to promote a reprint book club discovered that one of the books being offered to new members—a once-popular novel—was first written before World War I, when it had enjoyed a scandalous reception. In checking a bio-bibliography of the author, the copywriter learned that the book was actually a thinly disguised account of real life events.

This became the theme of her letter, a traditional "Did you know?" format that sold as it informed. By breathing new life into a rather dull assignment, she created a package that became a strong new-member promotion.

STEP 2. LEARN WHAT THE PRODUCT OR SERVICE IS EXPECTED TO DO

Develop a list of questions to ask everyone who may know something about what you're selling. Here are some sample questions you may want to ask, either in writing or in person or by phone:

- What is this product supposed to do?
- What does it actually do? How does it perform?
- Is it better than competitive products? Why? Why not?
- What do consumers want this product to do?
- Is it priced fairly?
- Is this an improved version? How so?

STEP 3. SELF-ANALYSIS: PUT YOURSELF IN THE USER'S SHOES

Write down the answers to these important questions:

- Who should buy this product?
- Why should I buy it?

- What do I think it's going to do for me?
- What will it actually do for me?
- What do I dislike about this product?

STEP 4. DECIDE WHAT THEME YOU'RE GOING TO EMPHASIZE

Evaluate your lists in relation to each other, to see if a concept or strategy springs to mind. Write yourself a little superscription or "Johnson Box" (a short message printed above the salutation), articulating the very essence and uniqueness of the product or servicer along with the key benefit and offer. Write a headline or envelope teaser around this idea. Is this the message you want to convey? Or has another idea come to mind? Very often, this kind of list making and headline writing will help you find the right direction.

STEP 5. PLAN HOW TO GET THE PROSPECT FROM YOUR OPENING PARAGRAPH TO THE ORDER FORM

1. *Map the sequence of events.* Develop a list of stepping stones, important ideas that will keep the prospect reading (and salivating). Check the lists you've made up. Are you pushing all the hot buttons that will sell your product or service?

2. *Note the debatable areas.* You have to anticipate questions or objections, because you're not going to be able to answer them in person. Prepare to answer them with graceful turns of phrase or thoughtful points that will further your argument rather than slow it down. Be alert to "clever" ideas that may only lead you up a blind alley. Does your sales argument flow?

3. *Chart your argument visually.* Design a step-by-step map that charts the sales points to be pursued—and avoided—on the way to the order.

4. *Note the important traffic lights and toll booths.* Plan to highlight in some manner the most vital parts of your sales talk. Use subheads, color, indented paragraphs, repetition, a second

voice for a radio commercial, superimposed titles on a TV screen, other similar devices.

Sales Promotion Ideas to Boost Catalog Pull

Even that powerful selling tool known as the catalog can show signs of battle fatigue. How do you counter competition, customer ennui, new trends, economic slumps, and direct mail overkill?

Armed with your knowledge of your customer and your products, look into some of the sales promotion ideas that may boost response.

1. For a clothing catalog, preempt the competition and become a fashion expert. Add service copy to your product description. Talk about styles and accessories, romance the history of fabrics, or trace the origin of the product's name.

2. Send a calendar to your customers every month, actually alerting them to your mailings rather than "surprising" them. Your regular customers have probably gotten used to your mailing pattern, but letting them know when they could expect the next mailing will be appreciated nevertheless. It'll be much like receiving a magazine on a regular basis, and it'll give them a chance to plan and budget for purchase. The calendar might also tie in interesting dates and holidays to your catalog. Formatted as a desk or pocket diary, it can be useful as well.

3. Encourage correspondence from your customers. This feedback can guide you in choosing new products, designing layouts, writing copy, and pricing your merchandise. Publish the best letters in a regular "Readers' Column." Offer a discount or a special on slow-moving merchandise to encourage letter writers.

4. Consider a joint mailing with a noncompetitive catalog marketer. Create synergy for both companies with this exciting "event." Ideally, your partner should have products that complement yours. For instance, a mail order photo-product house and an outdoors recreation supplier might do a mailing with a joint theme, an-

nounced in a letter signed by both companies, of "Cameras and Camping." Each catalog retains its identity, of course, with orders going their separate ways. However, a special joint offer could be made in the letter with a special order form at the bottom of the letter.

5. If you have a clearance mailing, sell by price rather than merchandise. Group all merchandise together by similar prices—a "save $20" or a "save $5" page—rather than in groups of similar goods. This also gives you the opportunity to offer two-fers or add-ons or "one-cent" deals.

6. Remember your regular customers with special discounts. Write to last year's best Christmas customers with an early-"snow bird" offer on your forthcoming catalog. Rather than cutting down your average return, it may build orders dramatically.

7. Use "magnetic" selling. Spot your best-selling products several times in several places throughout your catalog. Their proximity to other products will help boost sales of slower-selling items.

8. Be informative. If you're selling wristwatches, weave some romance into your copy. Tell the customer how your buyers make their purchases, how they travel to foreign countries in search of the "perfect watch." Show how a watch works, how to care for a watch, what to wear with a watch. An aura of objectivity and helpfulness can be very persuasive.

9. Invite customers to join your "panel of experts." Pretest products by asking these experts to vote on them, offering them a courtesy discount. Publish the most interesting comments.

Catalog promotions need not be elaborate or expensive. But employing some of the ingenious ideas that sales promotion specialists have dreamed up over the years can help you move more merchandise.

Use the Indirect Power of Parallel Marketing

Accounting software programs usually warn the new user to run a parallel double-entry system for the first six months or so, while breaking in the program. Keeping two sets of books means a duplication of effort, entering all figures on a computer while also keeping books the old-fashioned way.

Parallel bookkeeping is intended to be no more than a temporary failsafe measure and is probably more reassuring than realistic. However, there is another parallel business technique that is more like a four-wheel drive in its power and capability: parallel marketing.

Parallel marketing is the technique of turning traditionally non-advertising tools into powerful marketing devices. It was probably created originally to promote professional services without violating canons of behavior, or as a genteel way to sell products or services without seeming to be "commercial." It also plays an important role in goodwill promotions, public relations, and in business-to-government marketing.

Today, all kinds of marketers are using parallel marketing to enhance, or in some cases even replace, their advertising. The reasons? Advertising costs continue to climb, once-dependable media deliver inconsistently, competition for market share is heating up, and new opportunities for sales promotion remain elusive.

Basically, parallel marketing is a complementary technique that attempts to solve a marketing problem through *inference*, rather than head-on communication. The small retailer who gives away an extra service or product (the shoestore that gives you an extra pair of laces with a new pair of shoes) is practicing parallel marketing. So is the movie studio that conducts guided tours.

Here are some ways you can use parallel marketing in your direct marketing programs.

• *Professional promotions.* While restrictions on professional advertising have eased up in the past few years, many lawyers, CPAs, and physicians aren't enthusiastic about the kind of high-energy advertising retailers or manufacturers have used. For these shy but ambitious clients, you could create the offer of a free invitation to a professional seminar on tax reform (for CPAs) or on osteoporosis (for orthopedists). Hospitals might offer free courses in first aid, baby care, or weight loss.

• *Financial services promotions.* The idea of free seminars has long been used by brokerage houses and banks, but other industries can use them effectively too. A real estate company might run a seminar on condominium conversions for small-business owners worried about escalating office rents. Or a second-mortgage company might hold a neighborhood class on home equity loans. As a second-generation marketing tool, a professional seminar organization might offer a transcription or videotape to attendees, or to those who couldn't be at the seminar in person.

• *Personal service promotions.* In addition to seminars and courses, organizations such as driving schools, health clubs, and interior decorators can give away free booklets or offer an advice-by-phone service. The hallowed institution of demonstrations, a fixture of department store promotions since R. H. Macy greeted customers personally, can be extended to firms not usually known for their outgoingness. A title-search company can hold a class on local history for area bankers and lawyers. A newspaper might sponsor a reading by local authors for advertisers and their agencies. And a TV station might offer to videotape personal messages for its sponsors.

• *Business-to-business and business-to-government.* Sampling may be considered parallel marketing. It certainly is an established technique in direct marketing. But consider *inferential sampling.* For instance, the business supply house that gives office managers a complimentary copy of a book that extols new developments in filing. Or the scientific apparatus maker that underwrites a course in testing methods for veterinary technicians. Or the truck manufacturer that publishes a free newsletter on fleet management for county and municipal governments.

Parallel marketing may have been used by direct marketers in the past, but it deserves much more attention today as an attention-getting technique that can fuel a promotion.

Rules of Thumb for Direct Marketers

Rules of thumb, tips, surmises, and guesstimates are part of any good direct marketer's arsenal, ready to be used when the actual facts are imprecise—or intractable. These rules aren't exact laws, but, as Tom Parker points out in *Rules of Thumb* (Houghton Mifflin, 1983), they're not meant to be precise. They are guidelines evolved through shared experience and can help you handle a situation efficiently and with dispatch.

Direct marketing has been around long enough to have its share of received truths, which include these gems:

> If you want to use an attention-getter on the outside of the envelope, save postage by sending your message third class.—*Robert Collier*

> No product or service is a bargain at any price unless it is favorably known and a value has been firmly established.—*Bob Stone*

> There are six prime motives of human action: love, gain, duty, pride, self-indulgence, and self-preservation.—*Robert Collier*

> We consider each side of our envelope as another catalog page. That gives us two extra catalog pages.—*Jack Foster*

> Try phrasing your lead at least six different ways on the first sheet of paper you put into your typewriter.—*Maxwell C. Ross*

> Put an ad into an envelope just as it stands and it will not pull one-fourth as well as when split up into letter, circular, and order form.—*Robert Collier*

> Make the order form look too valuable to throw away, too valuable to waste.—*Henry Cowen*

You cannot hit a list too often. The only criterion is, will it pay out?—*B. L. Mazel*

The easiest person to sell books by mail to is one who has previously bought books by mail.—*Robert Collier*

Give me a good mailing list and I will find a product for it.—*Ellsworth S. Howell*

Whatever makes ordering easier helps results.—*S. Arthur Dembner*

Two order forms bring in more replies than the enclosure of only one.—*Edward N. Mayer, Jr.*

The closer the prospect is to the seller, the better the response.—*Maxwell Sackheim*

A charity organization would do well to pay as much attention to people after they have given money as they do before.—*Ernest Dichter*

Never use long words when short ones will do.—*William Cullen Bryant*

Your letter will account for 60 to 65 percent of the orders you get, your circular for 15 to 25 percent, and your order form for 5 to 10 percent.—*Robert Collier*

I look to products with a dream element. An exerciser, for example, which promotes the dream fulfillment of a better figure without putting forth much effort.—*Sam Josefowitz*

If you give your customer more than you promised, you build enthusiasm. And enthusiastic buyers are repeat buyers.—*Charles Andes*

Seven times out of ten, your average businessman will read the opening paragraph of a letter that is not from a customer, glance at the middle, and then jump to the last paragraph. Put a hook in your last paragraph.—*Robert Collier*

A good circular will add from 15 to 33 percent to the pulling power of almost any letter.—*Robert Collier*

I know of no mail order business that can survive without repeat business.—*Max Habernickel*

How to Create an Offer

Traditionally, offers have been constructed around cash rewards, but there are other kinds of offers that can enhance a direct marketing proposition. Here are some of the old and new ways of looking at an offer.

1. *The offer of reward.* You can offer either tangible or intangible rewards to a prospect. Tangible rewards may be money, discounts, bonuses, gifts, investment yields, or profits. Business-to-business promotions may offer loans, high net return, insurance, commissions, and royalties.

Intangible rewards include self-realization and improvement (often used in marketing correspondence courses and books). An adroit direct marketing practitioner can develop subtle nuances. For instance, seminars are often sold on the strength of their ability to develop people's skills on the job. Nothing is said about a higher salary for the better-trained worker, even though that pot of gold may be hinted at, pointed to, or reflected upon.

2. *Offer of nonreward.* This is the tactic employed by "last-chance" promoters. "This is your last chance to enjoy a 25 percent discount." "After the deadline, no more mortgage applications can be accepted at this low interest rate." "If we don't hear from you by the cutoff date, your name will be summarily removed from the register of subscribers." Nonreward or punishment can be as strong an offer as a reward; it's just not as friendly.

3. *The offer of authority.* Here's where an investment in corporate advertising can pay off. The marketer with a reputation for legitimacy, whether it involves a prompt refund policy or careful

descriptions of products, can extend this authority to an offer, either as a statement or as an implied benefit. Many established firms aren't aware of their special role in the marketplace and don't take advantage of their tradition and reputation, while new, unheard-of companies will attempt to create an air of legitimacy through dignified graphics, stilted language, and emphasis on a generous adjustment policy.

4. *The offer of security.* By bringing up problems of risk and uncertainty and offering a solution to these fears, an advertiser can often make more sales. Obviously mail order insurance programs hold out certain promises, but investments, real estate, and even job-related propositions can also use this offer successfully. The fear of remaining static while your peers climb has been profitably exploited by mail order home-study schools since the turn of the century.

5. *The offer of ease.* Making it easy for the prospect to order isn't often seen as an "offer," but it can drive in orders just as surely as a generous discount. Saving the customer steps, offering an 800 number, credit-card ordering, negative options, and automatic shipment plans can be powerful persuaders.

Can't construct an offer? Look again at every part of your product or service or distribution system. There actually may be several offers you can test! Creating an offer or proposition is an intrinsic part of any direct marketing effort. Unfortunately, it's often given short shrift. While not as glamorous as writing a piece of copy or designing an ad or creating a TV spot, building the offer should involve the creative staff as much as the "money managers."

Three Kinds of Offers

Over the years, direct marketers have evolved many different offers. Here is a list of possibilities that fall into three categories: (1) those that offer a discount; (2) those that provide financial help; and (3) those that offer a guarantee.

DISCOUNTS

• *Discount for cash.* This traditionally sturdy offer has always proved to be a good incentive and an eminently fair one.

• *Discount for quantity.* Obviously excellent for increasing the size of an order.

• *Free merchandise.* Yes, it's a discount offer. Instead of lopping dollars off the price of your product, just add on more product!

• *Prepaid shipping.* Today, when freight costs have skyrocketed, this can be an important consideration. Imagine an order form that boldly states "no charge" in the *add shipping charges* column!

• *Seasonal discounts.* Suggest that your prospects place an order before the Christmas rush or before spring planting to avoid delayed shipments . . . and also enjoy a price break "because we're getting a head start on our shipping."

• *Professional discounts.* This can be stretched to the limit. You can offer a discount to the accountant buying office supplies, to the pilot buying charts and maps, or to the librarian buying books. And also to the writer buying a typewriter, the music teacher buying a guitar, the kennel owner buying dog food, and the physician buying just about anything.

• *Discount substitutes.* Instead of cash or extra merchandise, offer technical assistance, an 800-number "hot line," a free training program with hands-on demonstrations, a subscription to a publication, a lifetime membership, or a "two-for-one" enrollment for a family member.

FINANCIAL ASSISTANCE

• *Seller-arranged financing.* For large purchases, your company might guarantee the lease or note. For small purchases, you can arrange for installment financing. How small can the purchase be to qualify for an installment plan? Today, even magazine subscriptions offer an interest-free, three-installment payment plan. From the very beginning, correspondence schools have offered a variety of tuition deals.

• *Trade-ins*. Rebates and credit arrangements can be generous, to encourage a prospect to buy the latest model and turn in last year's candidate for the scrap heap.

• *Extended dating*. First payment doesn't become due until some time in the future. And payments can be stretched out to match the prospect's budget and financial condition.

GUARANTEES

• *Free trial offer*. The customer can either pay up front or hold back payment until the trial period is over. One of the strongest offers you can make is a money-back guarantee with a healthy trial period. Mail order insurance companies spend a considerable portion of their direct mail packages extolling their free inspection offers (mandated by law).

• *Liberal return allowance*. Offer to pay postage and shipping on the returned item. You may be surprised at the rather small increase in the number of returns and the rather substantial increase in the number of orders! Offer a choice of cash or credit refund. Many more customers than you'd expect will take the credit and let the cash go. Some catalog companies sweeten the credit option by offering an additional percentage above the actual cash value of the returned item. However, they ask that the credit be used within a certain period, and they won't give the additional percentage in cash.

• *Reorder guarantee*. This "price protection" is especially strong in insurance, where rates can go up and up. But retailers of hard-to-find merchandise, magazine publishers, and service companies also use this reorder guarantee with good results.

You can also mix these discount alternatives, depending on your goals and requirements. Do you want a quick turnaround or are you looking for customers to stay with you? Are you promoting a lot of overstock items or do you want a good return business? Are you equipped to handle a fairly sophisticated discount arrangement, or would you prefer a COD procedure? Are the higher promotional costs worth the effort? And will you attract a quality customer who will remain loyal?

Design and evaluation of the offer strategy are vital parts of the direct marketing function. In addition to sweetening the deal, it can sometimes mean the difference between a great success and a mediocre effort. But caution is required: Cost out everything and weigh the consequences of an oversuccessful promotion where you may find yourself giving away the store. Knowing when to stop is also part of the creative effort, especially when crafting a good offer.

Increasing the Order With an Offer

There are at least seven good offers to choose from when you want to increase the size of an order.

1. *The good, better, best offer.* This highly successful offer is a well-known Sears device. You offer three versions of the same product or service. So a book club, for instance, may offer a standard edition, an expensively bound version, and a signed, limited edition of the same book. This choice allows the consumers, especially the irresolute, to enter into the fun of things by deciding which of the three they really want, rather than rejecting the product altogether.

2. *The deluxe offer.* This was probably the sire of offer no. 1. You give customers a chance to upgrade their offer with a gilt-edged, leatherbound book, or a subscription for twenty-four months rather than twelve. It doesn't cost much at all to implement. Just add a box to your order form, or tell your telemarketers to suggest the "deluxe" version. It's not even necessary to devote any selling space in your brochure or letter. The momentum that has carried

your customers from envelope to order form will continue to work for you and will often lead them into upgrading their order.

3. *Add-on offer.* Here again, all you need do is add a suggestion in the form of a checkoff box in the order form. Just ask the customer to buy something else after she's bought the chief product or service. It does help if the add-on has some association with the main product. Suggest a binder to hold the year's supply of newsletters, a software program to go with the computer, or leather soap for the expensive attaché case.

4. *Another product offer.* The multiproduct or multiservice offer's greatest manifestation is the catalog, but many successful ad campaigns have been built around a multiproduct effort. The laundry list of book remainders, hardware items, or close-out clothing can have the customer frantically adding to the original order. Try to avoid slight variations of the same product; they can make selection difficult.

5. *Piggyback offer.* This is a more subtle approach to the multiproduct offer. Make one product the hero of your ad or mailing but offer another product as well, perhaps in a flier along with your mailing or in a box in your ad. It doesn't even have to have a connection with the main product. Offer it as an inventory clearance or a "buyer's special" or "anniversary sale." It should be at a discount, though. You'll be surprised how much it can make the consumer like you.

6. *Extension offer.* While the customer's wallet is out, suggest an additional purchase linked to the original one. Another book by the same author, a gift subscription to the same periodical, a longer subscription period, the lady's watch in addition to the man's. A successful haberdashery has a thriving accessory counter. Consider the back of your brochure or the flap of your business reply envelope as your accessory counter.

7. *Bounce-back offer.* You've spent a lot of money to reach the customer and a great deal more to make the sale. Now is the

opportunity to make another sale, when the purchased item is in hand. Enclose a rebate coupon along with a mini-catalog tucked away in the set of luggage. Offer a set of bookshelves to the buyer of a set of volumes. Or a monographed eyeglass case to the customer who's just purchased expensive sunglasses. In fact, the bounce-back offer can be extended indefinitely to get as much mileage as possible out of the original purchase.

A Serial Seller Leaves a Sales Trail

Writing a series of collection letters can be as much fun as tap dancing on a high wire. The objective is to persuade a slow-paying customer who has hitherto shown no interest in writing checks to ante up some money.

Collecting a debt by mail can be an extended effort, sometimes calling for quite a few ingenious letters, which, of course, cannot be threatening or defamatory. In fact, both the stringent laws regulating collection efforts and a merchandiser's death wish to hold onto all customers, no matter how costly they may be, force a copywriter to be understanding, tactful, persuasive, brief, and sweet—in short, to go against nature. All of which is good total immersion training for *serial selling*—the art of extending a sales talk over a period of time.

The strategy of serial selling differs from the traditional "full-disclosure" (tell-to-sell) technique beloved of mail order practitioners. A full-disclosure direct mail package might include a four-page letter accompanied by a long brochure aided and abetted by a lift letter. Or an ad in small nine-point type might sprawl over two pages. Or a TV commercial might consume two minutes of the viewer's precious time.

Serial selling is different. For instance, serial selling in direct mail relies heavily on followup letters. Here, in answer to an inquiry, for instance, the first sales letter in a series would be involved and detailed. Then, in contrast, the next letter limits itself to a single benefit, the next one another benefit, and so on. The final "caboose" letter in this train might recapitulate all the benefits and make a strong, last-ditch effort to get the order, often through a surprise special offer.

Depending on the medium, serial selling uses variations on this followup technique. For instance, in a broadcast campaign, a long spot may lead off, followed by a number of short commercials each highlighting a single benefit.

A full-page heavy-copy ad in the front of a magazine may be followed by smaller or "teaser" advertisements in the back pages of the same issue or subsequent issue. (In contrast to "support" advertising, serial selling does attempt to make the sale in every exposure, rather than refer to a "master" commercial or ad or mailing the customer must order from.)

In serial selling, an elaborate mailing may be the first act of a number of lesser efforts—short letters, self-mailers, even postcards. Whatever medium is used, the format is usually the same: a "kitchen-sink" first effort followed by simpler single-benefit promotions.

Of course, campaigns often use serial selling in an attempt to stretch out a budget. However, rather than consider serial selling as a last-ditch solution to a tight money problem, think of it as a first line of defense, a practical technique whose components can blaze a sales trail and build a cumulative effect while working very hard to get the order.

Axioms of Direct Marketing Experience

Because so many people have worked in direct marketing over the years, and because, in the main, they've kept good records, we know what works and doesn't work, more so than in other areas of marketing. There are certain encapsulated axioms of experience that shrewd copywriters call on to simplify their task and polish their final product. Here are some of them.

• *Draw on any drawbacks and disadvantages the product may have when building your offer.* In addition to benefits, what are the problems? "Thinking negatively" lets you structure the offer in such a way that you can anticipate any problems or objections. If there are restrictions, special delivery charges, legal requirements, and the like, factor them in.

• *A sales letter need not be literal.* You don't always have to observe all the rules of letter writing when you're composing a sales letter. You may break the law with indentations, superscriptions, marginalia, underlinings, subheads, bulleted points, and a second color. The versatility of laser printing allows you to mix fonts and type sizes and do all sorts of other tricks as well. Not too many people today expect a sales letter to be a formal piece of correspondence, although there are times when breaking the law of the letter is tantamount to ignoring your audience.

• *In a two-step sale, intrigue and mystery work better than full disclosure.* For instance, when you're generating a lead, tell just enough to (1) qualify the lead (so you won't waste a salesperson's time), and (2) spark interest that will be sustained even when it's a long time between contacts.

• *Two work better than one. Three work better than two. Seven work better than six.* If you're planning a free gift or premium, consider giving away two cheaper items instead. If you use two examples, weigh in with a third. The "triad" serial device of listing things in threes gives a swing and beat to copy that is friendly, natural, and convincing. Odd numbers stick with the prospect; they may just skip over even numbers. So if you have to list thirty-eight reasons why, try for thirty-nine, or delete one and go for thirty-seven. Instead of a $4.98 price, make it $4.97 or $4.99.

• *Let somebody else tell your story.* If you can use testimonials or endorsements, take advantage of them. A third-party letter brings credibility that the most carefully reasoned letter from the owner cannot. A lift letter from a user with one genuine point to make can be more convincing than an elaborate brochure.

• *Create a club.* Consider making your prospects temporary members of an organization. Instead of trying to sell them an accident insurance policy, make them members of an affinity group created for the occasion, using your knowledge of them from the mailing lists on which you've found their name (business executives, alumni, homeowners, etc.). Instead of hawking a magazine subscription, offer it as the second or third benefit of membership in an ad hoc organization. (Other benefits may include handy ID card, magazine binder, framed certificate of membership, and discount rate for renewal.)

• *Use blank space.* Do you really *have* to put a teaser on the outer envelope? Can you substitute a musical "sting" for words in your radio commercial? Should your order card be jammed with an involvement device *and* a repeat of the company's address *and* a guarantee stub *and* a premium *and* a certificate border *and* a picture of the product *and* a restatement of the offer? Need every area in your ad call for a block of copy? Must your letter go on and on? Sometimes the meaningful pause can be as irresistible as words. And far more welcome!

A Mailing "Built for Two" Can Enhance Your Response Rate

In the metaphysical world of direct mail, two bodies can actually occupy the same space at the same time. What's more, they can often do more than twice the work they're capable of when acting alone! This supernatural feat is accomplished through *double mailings*—putting two separate enclosures from different people in the same package.

Thus, if you usually send a prospect a letter signed by your national sales vice-president, you might also include a second letter, signed by a local salesperson. This reinforcement of a promotion often results in a better pull than when a letter rides alone.

Here are several variations of this device that you may want to explore.

• *Co-op format.* Two marketers share the ride. The list may be supplied by a third party (a magazine or catalog company), and two catalogs, or two brochures, are enclosed. Taken to the *n*th degree, this co-op format becomes the very familiar card-deck mailing, in which twenty or thirty cards with different offers from different companies are mailed together.

• *Local retailer and national manufacturer.* Here, a local department store sends a mailing to its customers, including a second letter from a national company announcing a new product or an introductory offer. Each letter borrows strength from the other: the local retailer endorses the national manufacturer, the national company congratulates the local retailer's wisdom in carrying its line.

• *The carbon copy.* Years ago, when carbon paper and carbon copies were still to be found in offices, this was a favorite mailing ploy. In addition to the regular sales letter, a "carbon copy" (on very thin onionskin paper), supposedly from a company officer, would be enclosed. For instance, in a collection letter, the addressed letter would be from the president of the company, and the carbon copy would be from the company's lawyer. Together, these two missives would assault the recipient (sometimes in the familiar "good guy"/"bad guy" routine) and theoretically would make him cough up the owed sum sooner. Today, a photocopy stamped "COPY" in red ink might be used instead of a carbon copy.

The buck slip or publisher's letter is a variation of this device. The primary letter is signed by the sales manager or the editor and the buck slip (sometimes called a lift letter, because its use is supposed to lift response) is from the publisher or president.

• *One copy for you and one for your colleagues.* This is used in business-to-business sales efforts. Two copies of a sales letter are enclosed, with a little note suggesting that the recipient pass the second copy to a colleague who may also be interested in the proposition, or (tacitly) to somebody with the buying power that the original recipient may lack.

A variation is one letter for the secretary and one for the boss, to overcome the "gatekeeper" problem that too often holds back important sales material from the proper party.

Years ago, when homes were converting to oil heat from coal, an oil-furnace manufacturer might have sent two letters to the same household extolling his particular product, with letter A intended for the man of the house. The argument in this letter would be based on oil's lower maintenance expenses as compared with coal furnaces. Letter B would be for the wife, and its sales message would have dealt with such benefits as a cleaner house, quieter operations, and a surer supply of hot water.

• *Double envelope.* Here, two envelopes are joined along one side, with the contents of one intended for the addressee and the other for a colleague, associate, or partner. A variation could be the proxy mailing, where a smaller envelope is affixed to a larger one.

Like a double lift letter for those who have decided to say no and for those who have accepted the offer, this format is meant to so pique the recipient's curiosity that both messages will be read.

• *Endorsement letter.* A favorite of mail order insurance marketers, the endorsement letter usually comes from the bank whose credit-card list is being invited to buy health insurance. It repeats in softer language the offer being made in the letter from the insurance company. Or it may touch on neighborly themes that a big national insurance company may not be expected to know anything about—the recipient's excellent credit rating and special meaning to the bank as a good customer, and the bank's ceaseless search for ways to enhance credit-card membership. It is also heavily used by affinity groups to develop credit card membership.

• *Yes/No return envelopes.* Popular with sweepstakes promoters, this supposedly makes the life of the mailer easier, by having the recipient mail back an entry in one of two envelopes, either as a customer-plus-entrant or just as an entrant. But the use of two envelopes actually gives nonbuyers another opportunity to reconsider the folly of their ways, and they're apt to take up the offer and use the "Yes, send me a year of your magazine" envelope to enhance their chances in the contest, in spite of all the small print to the contrary in the mailing.

Does the use of a mailing "built for two" enhance response? In many cases it does. In others it can weaken or confuse the message, as well as increase the weight of the package. But in a discipline that uses split runs, two-step promotions, and the two-minute TV commercial, any mailing that attempts to sell twice as hard deserves a second look.

Direct Marketing Lessons From *A Book of Five Rings*

For a brief time, the Japanese martial arts classic *A Book of Five Rings* (The Overlook Press, 1974) enjoyed a vogue among American businesspeople who saw in it the source of Japanese business strategy. In Japan, entrepreneurs do turn to *A Book of Five Rings*— but as a psychological guide to strategy, not a sourcebook of strategic answers.

Originally written as a study of kendo (Japanese swordfighting), this 300-year-old guide is surprisingly relevant to any direct marketing operation involving plans and tactics. In its sometimes maddeningly elusive way, *A Book of Five Rings* offers the contemporary direct marketer certain insights into sales campaigns and marketing tactics.

• *Timing in strategy.* *A Book of Five Rings* emphasizes the importance of many kinds of timing. It speaks of "background timing"—which for a direct marketer can be the timing of a campaign set against the marketplace. For instance, how many new publications were capsized because the initial mailing hit mailboxes around April 15? Should your Christmas catalog be early or late, coinciding with the last wishbone of Thanksgiving or the first snow of December?

• *"Attitude no attitude."* Cutting through the philosophic fog surrounding this particular adage, one finds that a swordsman should never take a sword in hand without intending to cut the enemy. ("Attitude" refers to the way a sword is held.) In the same way, an ad should never be placed in a publication without a purpose—to sell. A mailing shouldn't be sent merely because competitors are mailing or because a budget has to be spent or because a manufacturer's cooperative allotment must be used up. To merely go through the motions is wasteful and, in the words of *A Book of Five Rings,* unharmonious.

- *"No design, no conception."* Acting calmly and naturally in the face of danger is the idea here. For the direct marketer this might mean handling the threat of unexpected competition without panicking. Should you abandon a campaign that has been carefully thought out because a competitor is using the same strategy? If a supplier fails to deliver on time, should you abruptly cancel an item or should you pursue other possibilities? If a description is wrong, do you acknowledge it in a letter or do you attempt to bluff or ignore it entirely?

- *"Crossing at a ford."* The swordsman is told to study the enemy's capability and attack his weak points, in the same way that a sailor will cross the sea. Emphasis is on bold action based on a complete knowledge of the situation. There are those who will act prematurely and those who will hesitate until it's too late. But to put yourself in an advantageous position requires firmness and thorough awareness. Will you mail with a complete understanding of every list? Or will you rent some names out of guesswork or just to use up an inventory? Do you find yourself using clichéd arguments in copy, or have you really done your homework and know which hot buttons to press?

- *"To become the enemy."* The swordsman who thinks himself into the enemy's position understands the enemy. It's an exercise of everyday empathy, but how often do direct marketers weigh the needs and wants of prospects? The very best copywriters imagine themselves reading their own letters, filling out their own order forms. And suddenly a difficult product becomes simple and a sales argument becomes apparent. In the words from the old comic strip "Pogo," "We have met the enemy and he is us."

Is *A Book of Five Rings* an appropriate manual for direct marketers? After all, a 300-year-old Japanese martial arts manual won't really add another percentage point to your results. But it can make you reflect on the techniques and tactics you are using to get business. Trying to apply military strategy per se to business is at best clumsy and tasteless and really has no place in commerce. But studying the ideas behind the strategy can often illuminate the dark corners of a problem far from the battlefield.

Should Your Promotion Push or Pull?

If you're a manufacturer, the chances are good that you are using an interrelated system of distribution to sell your products. For a large book publisher, say, this sequential, multistaged pipeline, or "channel of distribution" to the ultimate reader, may include wholesalers, large bookstore chains, individual bookstores, and other retail outlets such as stationery stores, Bible and church goods stores, hobby shops, greeting card shops, college stores, and department stores. They'll no doubt be selling through library distributors and directly to readers as well.

The flow of distribution to the consumer sometimes is a long channel, involving, as in the case of book publishers, a certain number of middlemen. In some other fields, there will be commission merchants, selling agents, brokers, and resident buyers. In still other cases, depending on the manufacturer's resources and needs, the characteristics of the product, and the number of potential customers, "zero stage" distribution system (which for many of us in direct marketing is the *only* system) makes sales directly to the ultimate user, or perhaps only to retail stores.

Quite often, the longer this hierarchal channel and the more stops between the manufacturer and the consumer, the more necessary it is for manufacturers to do their own heavy promotion. That's because the intermediary "way stations" are not usually enthusiastic about supplementing manufacturer promotion with their own, figuring it may help competitors too much. (Products that are *exclusively* rather than *intensively* distributed are the exception to this.)

The question for a manufacturer becomes one of push versus pull. If each middleman along the way has to be sold on the product (and the manufacturer) by the preceding one—for instance, the manufacturer promoting the product to the wholesaler, the wholesaler to the retailer, and the retailer to the ultimate user—the product can be said to be *pushed* through the channel.

While trade advertising is often used, direct mail can be an ideal medium for doing the pushing and generating the enthusiasm required at each step of the way. Using such offers as price-off deals, quantity discounts, and trade allowances, a series of letters from the manufacturer might be sent to *each* step along the way. In addition, the manufacturer can prepare form letters for middlemen to use in promoting to lower levels, all the way down to the store and ultimately to the consumer. A wholesaler might send a letter to the retailer, and the retailer might mail a prewritten promotion to its customers.

The offers may change along the way, but because the letters are emanating from the same source, identity and continuity will be strong and enthusiasm will be maintained throughout. (Also, details of the product can't be mangled by unknowledgeable writers along the way!)

As the promotion percolates down to the next level, the offers may include not only an elaborate, professionally prepared mailing but also a co-op deal, with the manufacturer paying for part of the mailing. In some instances, the manufacturer may even produce and distribute the mailing, using the wholesaler's letterhead. Finally, in addition to the usual sales promotion tools such as shelf-talkers (promotional pieces hung from the shelf in a store), signs, and handouts, the retailer may receive mailing tools. These include preprinted letters, postcards, and brochures, as well as radio scripts and advertising mats (and advertising allowances).

While the *push* strategy relies on the channel of distribution, the *pull* strategy goes *around* it. It addresses itself directly to the ultimate user, with the manufacturer hoping that the consumer will do the spadework and convince retailers to carry the product, and so on up the line. It is also a good mechanism for testing product, market, and offer. It can be targeted with pinpoint accuracy.

Here direct marketing (along with free-standing inserts and other support advertising, for instance) can carry cents-off coupons, premiums, and other offers. Quite often, a targeted, personalized geographical mailing will direct the recipient to a local retailer, and any coupons enclosed might be personalized with both the consumer's and retailer's names, a very strong response device. In this case, the action would be twofold: (1) purchase of the product with (2) endorsement of the coupons.

A combination of both push and pull strategies is used by most manufacturers. Introductory promotions, stocking, display and advertising allowances, and direct merchandising efforts must be entered in the mix. Combining the strategies with direct marketing tactics can go far to help you achieve your goals.

Extrasensory Perception and Direct Marketing Success

Practitioners of direct marketing aren't used to being referred to as paranormal, but any student of Dr. J. B. Rhine, the noted researcher of extrasensory perception, can certainly spot the similarities between a good direct marketer and the average "gifted" psychic. While there's no need to run down to your neighborhood exorcist for bell, book, and candle, you may find it instructive to look into "the ESP Connection"—the extrasensory perceptive skills every direct marketer employs.

• *Telepathy.* Reading your prospect's mind is good salesmanship. A good salesperson can interpret body language, responses to questions, and the hesitations and pauses of ordinary conversation in an almost occult way. But what if you're some distance from your prospect? How can you anticipate responses to your message? Answer objections so as to turn away wrath? Practice that good old empathy, which is nothing but a cousin of telepathy? The solution is, use the information you're privy to. Mailing lists or readership and audience studies can tell you a lot about your prospect, so you won't throw your net in a freshwater pond in an attempt to catch tuna. You can talk to your prospects using the right tone, style, and language that they'll respond to. And you can touch the "hot buttons" that will make them act because you know something about their lifestyle, purchasing habits, income level, occupation, and family size.

• *Teleportation.* The ability to move through time and space effortlessly has been given you, courtesy of the U.S. Postal Service. A good mailing piece is more than your ambassador, it is really a representation of the personality you want to set before the public. Tone, appearance, and presentation should mirror your company at its best.

• *Telekinesis.* Moving distant objects around is child's play for both poltergeists and direct marketers. Your telekinetic powers are being unleashed every time you make a prospect reach for a pen or a telephone or insert an order form into a reply envelope.

• *Clairvoyance.* This is the scariest paranormal gift of them all because it is so efficient. No myopic peering into crystal balls, no pushing around soggy orange pekoe tea leaves, no shuffling tarot cards. This is industrial-strength fortune telling. Extrapolating the results of a test and successfully predicting the outcome of a rollout are done on such a regular basis that we forget they're actually predicting the future.

The tools of your own trade can seem mundane and even quite dull, so it pays to step back every now and then and take a different look at what you're doing for a living. If not witchcraft, direct marketing certainly has an aura of wizardry about it. While the scientific community may still disagree as to the existence of ESP, we know that there are more things in heaven, earth, and a good mailing package than are dreamed of in the philosophy of the ad manager or sales promotion specialist who has not gotten around to using direct marketing.

Prudent Methods to "Cream" a List

In addition to building a mailing list through sales records, credit records, general correspondence, inquiries, requests, sales reports and recommendations, and publicity, there's the temptation to "cream a list." This is the practice of using a rented list to develop your own list, by making a premium or sample offer, for instance. (Some mailers will not allow their lists to be rented for offers of this nature.) The idea is to build up enough names on your list so that you don't have to pay a rental fee; eventually you can even rent your own list to other mailers! Another method is to hold a contest or a sweepstakes to garner enough individuals so that you soon have a sizable mailing list. Bingo cards and print ads that offer samples will also bring in a lot of names.

These methods are very expensive. Attractive self-liquidators or semiliquidators are few and far between, and the mailer usually has to make the sample offer at a loss. The prize, however, is a large mailing list. Is the effort worth it?

A mailing list made up of people who have asked for free samples, bought bargain premiums, or entered sweepstakes can be sizable indeed. But the buying power represented in this list is often minimal. Large-scale mailings to these lists aren't usually resounding successes for expensive items. However, cheap gadgets, imitation gemstones, inexpensive insurance, and even fund raising for obscure charities are possible propositions for these bargain-seeker mailing lists.

But surely all these names must be good for something, right?

One way to use them wisely is to set up a number of screens: criteria for judging the worth of names. Credit checks, demographic and psychographic analysis, and the rest of the armamentarium available in the form of sophisticated list overlays can help you locate individuals living in the "best" zip codes, potential deadbeats, coupon-clipping college kids, prison inmates, owners of fifty-foot cabin cruisers, and neurosurgeons who have taken two or more trips to the Grand Canyon in the last seven years.

Sadly, though, the *crème de la crème* will represent a tiny portion of your total universe. Carefully tracked offers made to your mailing list will tell you whether you have a white elephant, but meanwhile the list has to be supported: computerized, stored, kept up to date, added to, and so on. Is the effort worth it?

While it is tempting to build a large mailing list very quickly through the use of free offers, giveaway proposals, generous sweepstakes contests, and the like, experienced marketers proceed cautiously. Three of the methods they use to build large lists of good prospects include:

1. *Gifts tied into a product.* This qualifies orders or leads. When the Kaypro computer was originally offered in the early 1980s, it came "bundled" with a generous selection of software programs. A nucleus of loyal Kaypro owners was assembled, computer owners who later traded up to more advanced models.

2. *No free gift.* Sometimes the offer of a free gift can backfire, because of the suspicious nature of consumers who don't really expect to get something for nothing. Thus an offer of a free gift to announce a new store opening may draw fewer people than the offer of a generous discount on merchandise.

3. *Small initiation fee.* This token charge eliminates the curiosity seekers without driving away potential customers. There are many ways to position this fee: as a membership cost (for a discount merchandise-by-mail service), as an introductory subscription, or as a rebate-refund certificate.

While it's true that production costs are lower when you're mailing to a large list, that old back end will kick you in the teeth if you're not careful about the quality of your names. Creaming a list may have its attractions, but be aware that it may turn sour on you.

Attached Mail: The Lift Letter Achieves Grandeur

Lift letters, buck slips, or publisher's letters are small inserts added to direct mail packages. They are a comparatively recent addition to the direct mailer's armory. Because their ability to increase response in many cases has been proved in test after test, they are now often automatically included in every package.

Sometimes you'll find them casually dropped in, an afterthought on a slip of paper. Often they'll sit in their own little envelope, marked: "Don't Open Unless You Have Definitely Decided Not to Save $14" or some other accusatory message. They've also been clipped or stapled to the "big" letter or folded into the accompanying brochure. Sometimes they look like memos or telephone messages. And other times they're printed on personal or executive letterheads.

In the hands of a master, they can serve as a Greek chorus, commenting on the main thrust of the package and adding an objective note of endorsement. When used perfunctorily, though, they can be so casual as to be throwaways, neither impeding nor aiding the sale, just a component that's present because everybody is using it.

Up to now, the lift letter has been treated as an appendage to the package, but there is a way to put it in the limelight and allow it to act as a supercharger, boosting response higher than you might expect. It's expensive and, like all package enhancements, should be tested against a plain vanilla control. It uses the concept of attached mail but goes that postal delivery system one better.

Attached mail allows a first-class piece to ride along with a second-class, third-class, or fourth-class piece at the lower rate, provided its purpose is secondary to that of the host piece. For instance, an invoice can be sent with a magazine or merchandise and be charged at the lower rate. Often, this invoice will travel in its own envelope attached to the face of the host piece. This piggyback type of mailing is also used in proxy envelopes sent to shareholders where the whole package might go first class.

Interestingly enough, attached mail hasn't been used to a great extent in direct response advertising, where, because of its relative uniqueness, it may get noticed.

Instead of putting the sales letter in the ride-along envelope, which can be either open- or close-faced, put a variation of the lift letter in there. This time, the lift letter can raise the curtain, taking the place of an envelope teaser, in the same way that the buck slip or publisher's letter serves as an extension of the postscript. For a familiar name, such as a heavily advertised product or magazine, the lift letter can also serve as an "executive summary" of the direct mail package in the larger envelope and ask for the order, with the assumption that busy people will respond immediately and others will take the time to read the more elaborate promotion inside, or at least file it.

For a catalog house, the lift letter may be an order acknowledgment or an invoice accompanying a special large catalog for good customers. For a public television station, the small letter may be an off-cycle plea for more funds from members, with the large mailing a standard membership package, serving as a reminder. Mail order insurance can use the small letter as a wholly objective, third-party endorsement, completely segregated from the promotional package inside. Affinity-group credit card mailings can have prepackaged mailings with the group's endorsement riding piggyback as an attached envelope.

There is no postal savings involved, since it's not an incidental attachment but one that's primary to the purpose of the mailing. But by isolating and drawing attention to the lift letter, a component that is so often just taken along for the ride, you can turn this versatile little fellow traveler into a strong response engine.

Beware of Bronzing, or, How to Turn a Golden Offer Into Lead

When preparing a direct mail package, you want to make it as perfect as possible. This is only natural. You hope your package will pull like crazy, and it stands to reason that every component should be at its best.

Or should it?

There's a fine line between perfection and superperfection, and once you cross it you're in the realm of rigor mortis.

Inhuman direct mail, elegant and lifeless as a bronzed trophy, can be a fault of those who are expert in finding fault. While often associated with institutions of higher lending, ancient and worthy charities, and academic journals in the more obscure disciplines, the truly leaden promotion respects no bounds. It's the solemnly written letter that looks printed rather than typed, whose prose is embalmed, and whose pacing and rhythm are the envy of a military mausoleum's honor guard. You know that somebody has taken a calculator and counted the *thats* and *whiches*. And has blocked any attempt to indent blocked paragraphs, which are more businesslike.

It's the outer envelope without a teaser or legend, because that device is too promotional. It's the copy that tortuously avoids any first-person references, because Received Dogma says that *you* is the most important word in direct mail. And it's the diffident brochure that uses the latest, grayest, least readable sans-serif typeface for body copy because that's what all the great perfume ad designers are using these days.

But isn't it also true that there's too much sloppy, ill-conceived, poorly written, and atrociously designed mail being produced? Sure it is—direct mail is the most democratic of media. In direct mail there is no publisher or editor to demand that an outrageously ugly or offensive ad be pulled from the pages of the publication. And there's no FCC or station continuity acceptance department to ride herd over tasteless commercials. Within the bounds of postal regulations, in direct mail you can make a fool out of yourself however you please. After all, it's your postage. And the only censor is your bank when it declines to renew your loan, because you're not making the millions every direct marketer is supposed to harvest.

But as the vast majority of direct mailers can attest, you need not be a crude clown or an earnest bore to bring in orders. And if your mailing is in danger of entombment, there are several ways to open the window and let in some fresh air.

• *Practice enthusiasm instead of euthanasia.* In the belief that an innovative idea is dangerous, some mailers try to kill any sign of originality. However, to set your mailing apart from all the others and get it opened, read, and acted on, it's good practice to try for at least one new idea per package. Will it work? Test the idea instead of condemning it without a fair trial. The idea can be as bold as a letter written in a foreign language (with translation attached) promoting tourism, or as unrevolutionary as commemorative stamps instead of indicia. But as the gurus of brainstorming preach, "Don't edit." Give the idea its day.

• *Stammer instead of strut.* One of England's greatest orators held his audience enthralled in spite of a stutter. When asked if he found it to be a handicap, Winston Churchill replied, with no sign of hesitation, "Strangely, it comes and goes at the oddest times." He had found that instead of it being a liability, it caught the audience's sympathy and made them pay heed to his words. But stammering in print? Yep. There are letter writers who insist that no piece go out without one misspelling or typographical error. (Or so they say!) For years a successful mail order company ran ads that sounded as though a village auto mechanic had dictated them while on his second six-pack.

• *Be cool instead of cold.* Fred Astaire, that paragon of taste and style, never wore a suit without first throwing it against a wall several times. He knew that any store window dummy could wear a new suit, but to be worn well, it had to convey a sense of ownership and comfort. Consider the postscript that is "handwritten," the publisher's letter that is persuasive and personal instead of deadly dull, the brochure whose photo captions highlight benefits instead of describing obvious features, the promotion to older people that uses a larger, easier-to-read typeface, and mailings that empathize instead of emphasize. They may not fit all the rigorous standards and their apparent casualness may bother the person who goes by the book, but they have a glow and vitality that make them work. It is grace and elegance more than high-wrought faultlessness. It is integrity, common sense, and soundness. Consummate workmen, confident in their ability, know when to bend a little and add that little grace note of humanity that makes the difference between polite applause and a call to action.

The Untapped Wealth of Subscriptions

Wouldn't it be nice to have a customer all to yourself, without having to share him with competitors? Think of all that lovely business you could be doing, without fear of distractions or siren calls from other direct marketers, their noses pressed against your shop window, howling with frustration, and unable to break in and steal your customer.

Of course this is an exaggeration, but there is a selling method that for generations has been able to pluck customers out of the creek and set them high and dry, ready to be enjoyed by the shrewd marketer.

The method is well known: subscriptions. When subscribers enroll, they more or less take an oath of loyalty for a year or whatever the subscription term may be.

How is this oath of fidelity enforced? Through prepayment. Having a subscriber buy a subscription, the end of which won't be seen for a full year, means that you are both linked with a golden handcuff. While some subscribers—magazine junkies—will greedily graze on every offering in their mailbox, most will be content to take only one magazine in a subject area.

The tragedy is that most publishers don't take advantage of this special relationship. A golden year goes by and the honeymoon is over. With the exception of very early renewal attempts or some rentals to noncompeting firms, there hasn't been an attempt to exploit the reader's interest in the publication. How many special-interest publishers offer their readers book clubs and books, seminars, "hot-line" newsletters, on-line computer information services, conference boards and associations, affinity group insurance and credit cards, or cooperative buying programs? It's almost like sending out statement stuffers without the statements, deliberately walking away from a once-a-year opportunity.

Publishers will carefully explain that they are in the magazine business, not the merchandise-marketing business, and that their energies are devoted solely to their editorial product. But as a young Henry Luce said on the first page of his vastly entertaining and inspiring 1922 prospectus for a weekly news magazine, "*TIME* is interested—not in how much it includes between its covers—but in HOW MUCH IT GETS OFF ITS PAGES INTO THE MINDS OF ITS READERS" (*caps by Luce*). Surely, repackaging information and putting old wine in new bottles can make some of that information stick to readers' brains.

The subscription concept may be unappreciated by many publishers, but other organizations wisely use the selling structure of a presold, prepaid audience. Perhaps they can take advantage of the monopoly granted to them.

These include:

Museums
Subscription orchestras
Repertory theaters
Public TV stations
Charities
Membership organizations
Cable TV
Colleges and private schools
Chartered travel

Then, too, there are companies that can use the subscription concept as an alternative selling method. Book clubs might offer a year's paid-up membership at a discount to readers who are in the habit of taking all the selections. (Book clubs that sell reprints or specially commissioned books sometimes charge an annual subscription fee.) If FTC and postal regulations permit, book publishers might return to a traditional way of issuing books and solicit a subscription fee before publication. In the 1880s, Charles L. Webster & Co., a publishing company owned by Mark Twain, employed whole divisions of Union Army veterans to sell millions of copies of General U. S. Grant's *Personal Memoirs* door-to-door in this fashion. The book has been called the greatest nonfiction publication sale in American publishing history. And very costly works, such as Audubon's portfolio *The Birds of America*, could only have been completed with a subscription method.

Should the names of good customers simply rest in limbo, because their prepayment entitles them to freedom from solicitation? Insatiable marketers, ever on the prowl for sales, feel that no prepayment of any size can be great enough to buy this kind of privilege, and go about their selling with the enthusiasm of a wolf in a sheepfold. On the other hand, through carefully designed promotions that can actually enhance the value of a subscription by conveying a sense of exclusivity and selectiveness, the innovative marketer, who knows that the best customers are current customers, can tap this very special market without arousing the ire of the subscriber.

Use Ingenuity and Flair to Bring in Orders

It's very easy to fall into the trap of monotony when you're responsible for a great many direct mail packages. After a while, you may find yourself ordering up a standard format like a tunafish sandwich from a luncheonette menu: "Give me a six by nine window envelope, order card showthrough, personalized eight and a half by eleven two-page letter with blue sig, and a five by eight flier."

The word that should start the alarm bells ringing is *standard*. Even if the format has been shown to work, why not spread your wings a little and experiment, to raise the response rate a little higher?

Like it or not, your competitors are beginning to investigate interesting diversions such as popups, audio microchips, and poster enclosures. They may not be in the same business you are, but they are competing for the attention of the same reader. And sometimes a good offer, good copy, and carefully selected lists just aren't enough to do the job. But some ingenuity and flair may pull it off.

More than one hundred years ago, direct mail companies were using miniatures, samples, and dimensional objects as well as die-cutting and embossing techniques in an attempt to set their promotions apart from others—and this was in an era when the elaborate mailing campaign, though often carefully crafted and designed, was still in its infancy, and customers, no matter how jaded and bored, wouldn't throw away a piece of mail without at least perusing it.

A revival of a very old mailing device—the wax-sealed envelope—can still open envelopes. Designers don't seem to concern themselves with envelope flaps, which is a pity. Letter envelopes that open from the side rather than the top or are closed with string or tape can pique curiosity in a way that gummed flaps can't (and can rapidly age a production manager too; always look into the feasibility of a new idea before running with it!). And think about the possibility of using the flap side of an envelope as the address side;

all that unblocked space on the other ("poster") side can become your designer's playground.

And where is it written that a mailing tube must hold a poster or some other unfoldable or unbendable object? Why not use the tube as an interesting outer envelope to be stuffed with a letter, order form, BRE, brochure? *Important:* Make sure the tube can be opened by anybody not near a fully equipped mailroom.

There are even opportunities to create your own envelope. For instance, a cardboard laundry shirt stiffener can be pressed into service, if you wrap and laminate an illustrated die-cut sheet around it and the contents (leaving room for address and indica).

Instead of paper enclosures, think of the possibilities that fiberglass, Styrofoam, and other plastics offer. Print a message on the back of an 8 × 10 photograph. Book publishers sometimes run off extra copies of a book jacket and print their promotions inside, but not too many think of using the galley-proof format as a promotion media, even though a galley proof is a rather interesting sheet of paper, especially to people in the book trade.

A participatory device may also be used. Some stage productions allow the audience to follow the action by actually walking through sets and keeping up with the cast as they move through different rooms. Why not borrow this idea by telling a story through various office forms?

For instance, a series of reproduced telephone message forms can tell the sad story of somebody who kept on missing important messages because of poor time management. An insurance mailing might include copies of actual accident claim adjustment forms and payment checks. Facsimiles of frighteningly large hospital bills have been used by hospitalization insurance companies. And somebody offering a surefire order-tracking system can strike terror in the heart of any manufacturer by sending copies of purchase orders, repeated requests for shipment, and cancellations. A playlet in an envelope can be a dramatic art form.

Even *considering* an unexpected component in a mailing can make you think twice about what you are about to do. You may never actually go through with the elaborate (and, yes, expensive) production of a curiously interesting insert, but you've broken through that barrier that separates the innovative from the routine, and that in itself can lead to creative marketing.

CHAPTER 4

Achieving Maximum Profits

The First-Time Mailing: Is It Ready?

Before you invest time, labor, and money in a first-time mailing, you may want to assess its feasibility. Of course you can always do a test. But there are certain conditions and items you can use as informal and inexpensive checkpoints to see if a project is really practical before committing yourself to it.

There are four areas to investigate.

1. CONCEPT AND QUALITY

Do you know enough about what you are selling? Can you write a brief sentence—a headline—stating the offer and most salient benefit? Have you enough information about the market? Can you justify offering the product or service to a particular audience? And do you have a Big Story, an orchestrated concept that is built on a thorough command of all information?

Doing a mailing without having all the facts at hand is like going into battle without having scouted out the enemy. What about the quality of your data? Is it accurate, reliable, valid, and up-to-date? Do you know everything there is to know about the lists you may use? Have you weighed possible inconsistencies in marketing analysis, such as purchasing patterns that don't seem to jibe with demographics, or a curiously disproportionate mixture of TV-watching habits and leisurely activities (doesn't anybody work in that neck of the woods?). Are there unanswered discrepancies concerning historical sales figures versus current experience? If you're writing copy, do you know the product inside out? What gaps of knowledge yawn wide?

2. CONTEXT AND CREDIBILITY

This concerns the meaningfulness and practicality of your offer, *as perceived by your prospect*. If the recipient of your mailing isn't able to find a *real benefit*, you're just whistling in the wind. Incidentally, a benefit need not be a tangible dollar gain. It can be a challenge, as with a political or fund-raising effort ("Are You Big Enough to Face Up to These Problems?"). Or it can even be a provocative idea ("Test Drive the Brand-New Gizmo, Even Though You've Just Bought Yourself Another Car"). But whether it's a challenge, gain, or provocative notion, it had better be a benefit that will keep your reader interested.

The believability of your offer will also affect results. Are you fighting an uphill battle because of obscurity or a tainted past? Is your company brand new and unknown? Or does it have a history, deserved or not, of reneging on promises? Is the product or service gimmicky or solid? Is pricing realistic?

And is your proposal coming at the right time? Credibility is often a matter of good timing. Holding a cents-off catalog sale on the heels of local retailers' January white sales is unfairly handicapping yourself. Are you selling cable TV at the start of the summer, when people are thinking "outdoors"? Or do you intend to promote a precious-metals mutual fund in the face of a boom in municipal bonds or common stock?

3. CAPITAL AND COSTS

Do you have the budget for a well-planned, well-executed mailing? Or will you have to shave expenditures, often at the last minute and often in vital areas? Could you roll out without depending on a "bootstrap" operation, where revenues from the test mailing are expected to fuel subsequent mailings?

4. COORDINATION AND CONFLICT

Have you scheduled print or broadcast advertising in support of a mailing? Has the sales force been alerted if you're doing a lead-generation program? Will vacation schedules, off-premises conferences, or sales trips of key decision makers interfere with mailing plans? Will your mailing need legal clearance, and have you allowed enough time for possible revisions? Have you spoken to the postal authorities about any required permits or possible extra manpower needs? Will the mailing interfere with any other planned promotions? Will branch offices find out about the mailing from clients, or have you planned an early internal communications program to alert all departments?

Is fulfillment firmly in place? Is there sufficient inventory to meet needs? Are there people available to answer phones and handle correspondence? Have suppliers been alerted? Will you be able to go back into the mail with a full-scale campaign as soon as possible to capitalize on your timing? If rewrites or new layouts are suddenly required, do you have the staff standing by? Are your computers on line?

Going into the mail in a mindless way is futile and wasteful. A half hour going over the pros and cons of a planned campaign can save many hours spent later trying to undo the effects of a hasty, ill-planned mailing.

Keep Your Eye on the Details

No matter how imaginative and innovative an ad, a mailing package, a commercial may be, attention must be paid to the 1,001 details making up your promotion. A great designer like Frank Lloyd Wright, for instance, may have created astonishing buildings, but these buildings are organic entities whose components were also carefully integrated.

Frank Lloyd Wright was a great architect, but we should remember that he was also a great engineer. From his Imperial Hotel in Tokyo to the country house "Fallingwater" and the Johnson Wax Building in Racine, Wisconsin, Wright's structures *worked* as exceptional constructions.

How can you get your direct marketing creations to work? By paying close attention to the details and minutiae.

• *Engineering.* Will the name and address of the recipient show through the window of your envelope, or will something be lost? Why not construct a dummy before spending a lot of money correcting mistakes? At the same time, weigh your package; are you going to be penalized for going over the limit? Try inserting the folded contents; have you devised some devilish accordion folds that no machine can handle? And don't forget to set up the proper order of the contents. Do you want your letter to be seen first? Or should it be the order form?

• *Endurance.* Will your ad last or is it fated to bloom briefly and die? Copy should not be so time-and-place specific that it is unusable at a later date in another market. Try for the eternal verities rather than current pop slang or fad (unless you're selling a product or service that is itself a seven-day wonder or feeds off a quicksilver trend). Leaf through some old magazines and notice how the really well-designed ads can still be used today while "pop" graphics and cute copy have made dinosaurs of other ads.

• *Endings.* Are you guilty of "false" endings—closing before you've concluded? Sometimes when we're pressed for space or time, we're apt to stop selling and say farewell, rather than allowing the message to end naturally or winding up with a logical call to action. While overstaying your welcome is a lapse, rushing off before you've made a sale is a sin. Diagram your ad, letter, or commercial to make sure that you're not cheating yourself and leaving out the best part—the true ending.

• *Energy.* A two-minute TV spot or a full-scale major-encounter type of mailing can be tiring to the creator as well as the prospect. Don't let it show. Make sure your promotion radiates energy. Don't use a spokesperson who lacks stamina and begins wilting on camera. Don't save your best for your brochure and let your letter limp along from a wimpy opening to a wishy-washy closing.

• *Enjoyment.* Does your promotion give the impression that it was written under duress? Does it resemble a product recall notice? A warm, pleasant tone can mean the difference between an enduring relationship or a permanent alienation. A discordant layout, unattractive pictures, inappropriate music, a preachy tone can give the most beneficial and useful product a bad name. No salesperson was ever hurt by having good manners and a pleasant attitude.

• *Environment.* Are you in the right pew? Is that very expensive mailing the right vehicle for a practical, serviceable, economical product? Is that elaborate brochure going to sell health insurance? Is that long-winded and exceptionally technical ad the correct way to sell designer jeans? Have you accurately matched up market, medium, and message? Or are you cluttering up the environment with aural and visual static?

Faced with awesome deadlines and unbelievable pressures, we sometimes fail to pay attention to the fine points of a promotion, with the result that the job "gets out"—but falls on its face. Before letting a promotion leave your hands, play inspector and test it with a clean white glove. You'd be surprised at the number of details you can improve, thus making your mailing, ad, or commercial powerful and cost effective.

Direct Marketing the Old-Fashioned Way

It may come as a shock to direct marketers used to thinking in terms of megabucks and stretch limousines, but there was a time not too long ago when direct marketing had to use the service entrance.

That was when direct marketing was thought to be a rather raffish means of unloading seedy merchandise on an innocent populace. Now that it's a respectable form of marketing, and demographers and market psychologists and socioeconomists are beginning to be seen in the reception areas of even the seediest mail order companies, it may be worthwhile to look at that old service entrance and the ways the old mail order entrepreneurs managed to get the attention of their customers.

"YOUR KIND HAS TO GO TO THE BACK OF THE BOOK."

Just a few years ago mail order ads were relegated to second place in a magazine, the publishing equivalent of a restaurant table somewhere near the kitchen: the back of the book. Today, of course, with even the *New Yorker* accepting coupon ads, the once-snubbed mail order practitioner is moving closer to the Front of the Book.

Now, we're not too sure that being up front is all that good, in spite of what readership studies say. Any observer of business knows that the companies that have traditionally stayed with two-inch ads in the back of the hunting, fishing, fraternal order, and do-it-yourself magazines have remained solvent and prosperous, while the four-color double-spread advertisers up front have come and gone so quickly that their trademarks have become synonyms for instability.

Lesson No. 1: Stay small and humble, and you'll stick around longer. Lesson No. 2: Try to swing a per-inquiry advertising deal wherever possible. Instead of paying for advertising according to a printed rate card, you pay for each response received.

"YOU CAN HAVE YOUR PARTY AFTER THE BIG SHOTS HAVE LEFT."

Prime-time television may be comfortable for soft-drink companies and fast-food chains, but when it comes to getting the viewer to exercise his credit card, there's nothing like hanging out between reruns of *M*A*S*H* and *The Bob Newhart Show*. Nothing, perhaps, except tagging after cable TV revivals of *Duck Soup* and *Gunga Din*. Nothing you can brag about at college reunions, but bankers do smile when contemplating the statements of broadcast direct marketing firms.

There still is a market for "50 Golden Treasures of Boogie Woogie." At three in the morning, you can board a time machine that actually works. Somewhere in the world of TV you'll find every old promotion ever made. It's like suddenly encountering that old corner candy store that you could have sworn disappeared during the Kennedy administration. Lesson No. 3: Carefully analyze the reasons otherwise sensible businesspeople seem ready and willing to hawk merchandise to insomniacs—and go thou and do likewise. Lesson No. 4: When a fancy production house recommends a six-figure budget for your TV commercial, ask yourself how many sets of china and cookware their last commercial sold.

"THE POSTMAN ALWAYS RINGS TWICE, JUST LIKE A CASH REGISTER."

Imaging, fancy folds, and personalization of everything including the postage indicia are the order of the day. But everything is still sent via third-class mail. Notice that term *third class*. Somewhere below the salt. Doctors don't send their bills that way. Nor do lawyers. But companies hawking their merchandise still feel impelled to send their catalogs that way.

And heaven help them if they abandon their parsimonious ways! Or omit mailing to their present customer list (sorry, database) in favor of a divinely ordained compilation of names. Lesson No. 5: Don't fly first class when you know that economy class will get you there at the same time.

While selling is not entirely a matter of "Upstairs Downstairs" dichotomy, it does behoove direct marketing people to remember their roots and ask themselves occasionally if some of the traditional methods, though not quite elegant, may be more effective, efficient, and economical.

How to Sell Quality in Direct Marketing

How do you support a claim of quality in your direct mail or print? If challenged, could you prove your claims? Making a statement on quality or performance can be interpreted as an implied warranty. To make sure your copywriters do not make unwarranted claims, provide them with the basic facts and specifics that will let them make valid and informed statements about quality. Some useful specifics that can back up claims of quality, maintainability, and reliability follow.

1. *Actual performance or reliability statistics.* These may have been gathered by outside observers or government agencies as well as in-house engineers, technicians, or other personnel. If citing track records in financial marketing—mutual funds, commodities, newsletter predictions—you should be aware of the very strict Securities and Exchange Commission regulations governing use of these past-performance statistics.

For instance, Rule 134 of the code of the National Association of Securities Dealers, interpreting the Securities Act of 1933, says: "A statement could be misleading because of representations, whether express or implied, about future investment performances, including representations implying that future gain or income may be inferred from or predicted based on past investment performance or portrayals of past performance, made in a manner which would imply that gains or income realized in the past would be repeated in the future."

2. *Notable improvements in performance or reliability statistics.* Best illustrated with charts. For dramatic emphasis in a brochure, you may want to consider using transparent overlays.

3. *Comparisons with competition.* Works best when you're number two in your field. Ignore the competition if you're the leader, unless you're far ahead. You can also use the competition's performance if you're selling something that's not usually compared, such as recipes, book clubs, or real estate. Selective comparisons may

work, if not too obvious. Don't "win" everything. Come in second in one or two categories to lend veracity. For instance, when comparing different types of investments, have your product or service falter in something like liquidity, if research shows this is not a prime concern among your customers.

4. *Endorsements by outsiders.* Testimonials work best if a certain amount of expertise is implied. Football players lauding new varieties of roses just aren't convincing. However, TV personality Art Linkletter as a spokesperson for National Liberty was very convincing, so an endorser with the right charisma might do well, no matter what his background. Any connection between the endorser and the product or service should be fully disclosed. The fact that Linkletter was a National Liberty board member "with a financial interest in the company" was a prominent part of all promotions.

Beware of using unsolicited testimonials without getting clearances. Federal Trade Commission guidelines are tough when it comes to testimonials and endorsements. They must be supported and real, and they cannot be worded or presented out of context (as is so often done with movie reviews).

Incidentally, while diamonds are forever, endorsements are not, which means you have to go back and check occasionally to see if the endorser is still happy with the product. Laypeople should not be used in drug promotions. And Consumers Union reports are usually off bounds. Very technical endorsements can also be a waste of space, unless you're allowed to translate the endorsement and tell the reader in simple terms what it means.

5. *Awards or commendations.* If strong enough, an award could well be the theme of the promotion. For instance, a series of Oscar-winning films made into videotapes. Or a continuity series featuring Pulitzer Prize–winning novels. Instead of the usual buck slip, enclose a facsimile of the certificate that comes with the award. The gushing praise of these documents is fine because it comes from an authoritative third party.

Is Your Mailing Fit Enough to Survive?

Why do so many mailings fall by the wayside? Is it the competition from other media or have mailings become flabby, overweight, weak? Perhaps an examination of your mailing from the standpoint of health and fitness may give you some ideas on how to improve it and help its standing next time it's mailed.

1. *Is your mailing too fat?* Are there actually too many pieces for the reader to wade through? Too much verbiage? Too many ideas? One big concept or theme is enough.

2. *Is your mailing awkward?* Some packages resemble fast-growing adolescents who are all legs, arms, and cracking voices. There's a sense of ill-preparedness, as though the mailing hadn't been thought through or had been put together at various times by various hands. Give your mailing the litmus test of consistency. Is it running smoothly and are all parts pulling their weight?

3. *Is your mailing inflexible?* Is there a stiffness, a lack of warmth about the package? Have you explored every possibility of selling? Or are you working with a rigid formula that won't allow you to stretch your imagination? If athletes don't build up their heart and lung capacity, the extra effort needed at the very end isn't forthcoming. And a mailing without a "second wind," without a powerful thrust, may not be able to cut it when it comes time for a buying decision.

What would this flexibility, extra capacity, or second wind look like? It may be a buck slip that answers anticipated objections and "turneth away wrath." Or a suggested alternative use for a product, like a mailing for a portable radio that offers a discount for a second radio to be sent as a gift.

4. *Does your mailing betray a lack of exercise?* Are you using tried-and-true but very, very tired techniques? If so, you're doing yourself an injustice and guaranteeing an indifferent result. If you try to add something special to each package, you're building up your own conceptualization strength, actually stretching your idea muscles. And a stronger creative ability can come in very handy when you're suddenly faced with a difficult assignment on short notice.

5. *Are you cutting corners without adding strength?* If you are faced with the need to cut down a mailing because of budget restrictions, don't just cut fat. Combine a flab-loss program with strengthening exercises. Instead of four colors, consider an unusually colored stock. Instead of an 8½ × 11 letter format, use a 5 × 8 sheet. Combine the letter with the order form, which shows through the envelope window. Combine the letter with the brochure as a four-page folder, with the letter on the first and last pages. These exercises in economy need not be humbling; they can improve your imaginative skills even as costs are lowered.

6. *Is your mailing pushing too hard?* You may be working against too much resistance and causing marketing strain. While most mailing goals are probably set too low (after all, a 97 percent failure rate would probably not be accepted in most other businesses!), you can sometimes ask your mailing to do too much.

☐ Are you selling too many products in one simple mailing?
☐ Have you overpriced your product?
☐ Are you timing the mailing to coincide with tax-return or vacation time?
☐ Do you have too many things happening at once in your mailing?
☐ Are you introducing a new book club with exotic titles that haven't been reviewed or talked about?
☐ Are you proposing a new service along with a complicated rate structure?
☐ Are you simultaneously preaching and trying to raise funds?
☐ Are you asking an untried list to deliver more than it has in the past?

Don't make your mailing struggle. Experiment, and then adjust the package. But don't push too hard—it can injure the mailing and its results.

7. *Is the mailing healthy?* Is the concept strong enough? Better yet, is there a concept? Many mailings lack theme, motif, or center. They leave the reader confused. Are there any weak spots that might

be better off eliminated? Does the envelope legend force too much, give away the story? If you've used a Johnson box, is it proclaiming or promoting? (The use of a superscription often becomes a reason for a pseudoheadline rather than an intriguing invitation.) Does the postscript further the story, encourage the order, or merely restate the obvious? Is the mailing truly ready for competition, or is it a last-minute substitute?

Storybook finishes happen only in storybooks. Your package must be world class to win in today's marketplace. Consider a mailing as an organism that must be strong and healthy to succeed. Does it have the stamina and tone to overcome reader inertia? Then put it in competition, mail it, and may the best package win!

Failsafe Mailing Packages

Once your package is launched, it's hard to rectify any mistake, so it may pay to apply the lessons of reliability engineering to your next effort.

Reliability engineering is an aerospace engineering discipline based on the reliability of a system's individual components. In short, a package is only as strong as its weakest component.

There's even a law (Lusser's Product Law of Reliabilities) that studies the product rather than the average of the reliabilities of the components making up the package. With this gauge you get a better evaluation of the weaknesses of each component, which can't hide behind the strengths of other components.

A very strong letter, for instance, cannot counterbalance a very weak brochure. A package consisting of a powerful offer that works 90 percent of the time and a brochure that has been a component of other mailings and has worked only 20 percent of the time has an overall reliability of only 18 percent.

It's inevitable that not every component in a package will pull its weight. Even in the most skillfully prepared mailing, there may be a weak link. Therefore, you should prepare yourself by trying to prevent package failure even if component failure—a confusing brochure, an unconvincing letter, or a hard-to-fill-out order form—occurs.

Aerospace engineers improve a system's reliability through "redundant design," adding in a second, buttressing component. In your mailing you can build in standby components that can take over if another component lets you down. For instance, if your four-page sales letter carefully builds a marvelous rationale for prompt action and then omits a deadline, your order form can supply that missing link. If your brochure has no price in it, deliberately or not, your personalized sales letter, order form, or drop-in notice can pinch hit.

What is important is that both standby and operating components are in place and that you have thought of all eventualities. Since direct marketing doesn't permit real-time telemetry (measurement at a distance) with subsequent adjustment, you have to be prepared in advance for all eventualities. You can't suddenly pull a mailing out of the letter carrier's hands and make the corrections.

Well, how do you weigh the comparative reliability of components? Through testing. Testing, which so often involves only "big-picture" thinking, can also be used effectively to measure the contribution of each component.

Examine each package's components carefully. When results are known, replace only one component and then analyze the new numbers. Was it the letter that worked most effectively? The list? The offer? Could the order form reinforce the sales message better? Should personalization be dropped? Is this piece going in because it's part of a formula, or will it help the package sell better?

Engineers "burn in" and "debug" components. "Burning in" means trying the component out in actual operation. "Debugging" involves repairing anything that goes wrong with the component when it is first used. You can do the same with your mailings.

To continue the parallel, it's important to prevent wearout by replacing components before they fail. A tired offer or brochure with a dated photograph may be holding back the success of the package.

To prevent failure, institute a checkout procedure. Careful analysis of each component will improve package reliability. You need a clear idea of what every component in a package should do, and you need to back up the other components. You'll feel better mailing a package when you've put a failsafe system in place.

Think Smaller for Bigger Results

For many direct marketers, a piecemeal concept instead of a broad-scale program may be more profitable. Instead of "thinking big," they're limiting their horizons while actually raising their sights.

For instance, mass marketing, a buzzword for at least twenty years, is now being reexamined by the traditional heavy hitters, who once thought nothing of saturating a huge total universe at once with mailings in the millions. Tinier chunks of the market-place, meticulously carved-out segments, appear to be easier to handle and manipulate, as witness Sears's born-again emphasis on special-interest catalogs. It's true for other businesses as well. Budweiser, commanding 38 percent of the U.S. beer market, prefers to operate in neighborhood segments.

A scalpel rather than a cleaver can be used in other areas besides lists.

PRICING

Instead of selling a one-year subscription for $24, offer it for $2 a month. The annual rate then sounds like a very convenient way to pay for a rather inexpensive deal. Instead of $25 for a 500-page book, position the price as $0.05 per page. Instead of $1,300 for a 640K computer, offer it for $2 per 1,000 bytes of memory. Instead of $60 for a month's support of an overseas orphan, restate it as $2 a day.

CREATIVE

Long, long letters can still work if done right, but you might want to be sure of keeping your reader's attention by extracting some of the juicy but slow-moving parts and printing them separately in a memo, brochure, or flier. For instance, when describing a coffee-table book, you may want to go into the romantic details of its actual production in a separate flier.

Another device is the second letter. Take a leaf from the mail order insurance promoter's book. The second or endorser's letter can take aim at statements that may be inappropriate in your main letter. For instance, a letter signed by the president or chairman of the board might not stoop so low as to mention price, but a second letter from the sales manager can be commercial. And if you have material left over for a *third* letter, use a lift letter. Of course, you can test all these components separately or together.

GRAPHICS

Instead of putting all your pictures in one brochure, consider a number of 8 × 10 captioned fliers. Or create your own deck of response cards, each with a variation on the same theme. Analyze the results to see which variation worked best and do a full-blown campaign based on that subtheme.

Fragmentation of a direct marketing program may seem like an inefficient way to put across a message, but, like market segmentation, it may prove to be a more effective tactic than the traditional all-or-nothing mailing. Small can really be better, as well as beautiful, when it comes to person-to-person marketing.

Ten Ways to Revive a Sagging Campaign

Are your direct mail campaigns sagging in the middle? Frequently, a campaign starts off with a big bang and then drops off, only to be revived again toward the end, because the direct marketer, as is so often the case, saved the best story for last.

However, there are at least ten ways to maintain continuity, interest, and a high level of performance in a campaign or series, whether you're trying to revive subscriptions or beat down the door for sales leads.

1. *Use your good packages again and again.* Slip a lift letter into the followup mailings, saying something like: "In case you missed this . . ." There's no reason to change for the sake of

change. Let your results, not your instinct, tell you when your package is no longer useful.

2. *Change the copy very slightly.* For instance, change the sequence in which you list benefits. Add subheads or discard them. Change the salutation. Add or modify the Johnson box superscription above the salutation. Consider a trial close. Modify the paragraphing. Add a second color. Important: Try not to alter the original concept, because your campaign should hinge on this theme.

3. *Change the format.* If you've been using a long letter, condense it into a shorter one, perhaps one sheet printed on both sides. Do you really need that broadside? Consider making it into a folder. Or turning the folder into a letter. Or eliminating the circular or broadside altogether.

4. *Change the timing.* Perhaps you've planned too carefully and your mailings are arriving like clockwork—or as close to clockwork as the postal system will allow. Introduce the element of the unexpected. Bunch two mailings together to arrive a day apart, or even together. Also, a mailing that arrives near payday may have a better chance than one that arrives when all the bills have been paid and there's nothing left in the family exchequer.

5. *Change the color of the paper and the ink.* While color can enhance results, you don't really know *which* color works best until you try it. Consider scented paper, popups and popouts, bulletin slips, and jumbo sizes.

6. *Modify the envelope, by changing shape, size, or color.* Add a legend (or delete the present one). Consider odd envelopes, like Tyvek paper, wallet flap, or two-compartment envelopes.

7. *Use another indicia.* Try precanceled stamps or a meter imprint, or modify the design or color of your present one within postal regulations parameters. Consider other postal maneuvers

such as endorsements ("First Class Mail" or "Postmaster, handle in accordance with PL&R").

8. *Shake up your mailing list.* In a business mailing, address mail to another title, the sales manager instead of the marketing manager, for instance. Or mail to both.

9. *Give something away.* Offer a premium. And change the premium offer frequently, since the more you change it the more times you can go back to the same list.

10. *Send a gift.* Consider using advertising specialties. An imprinted ballpoint pen may seem dull and hackneyed to you, but it's always a useful gift and a reminder of your name.

Sometimes a long, drawn-out campaign fails because everybody concerned is tired of it. Perhaps the campaign was too long to start with. Or wasn't planned carefully enough. But when results start to droop, don't give up hope. Instead, see how your story can be better told or brightened up or dressed up with a change of pace—and keep those letters coming.

Options in Direct Mail "Circulation"

Rather than think of direct mail as a single form of circulation—letters sent to names on a mailing list—look at it as a form of circulation that gives you many options. In that way, you may be able to come up with brand-new mailing concepts, based on a wholly different way of looking at your audience.

Using the circulation terminology of magazines, you can think of direct mail as a medium with several kinds of readership.

• *Paid circulation.* Direct mail as "paid" circulation? Who would pay to receive mail? Book-club members. Think of the membership as a group of people who have sent you a dollar or two in order to get on your mailing list, and furthermore have contracted to buy a certain number of books a year through your direct mail offers. The book club is the hottest of hot mailing lists. It's like charging admission to a department store where each visitor promises to buy a certain number of items before leaving.

• *Controlled circulation.* Publications distributed free to qualified readers are said to be *controlled.* The equivalent in direct mail are mailings targeted to a professional audience. For instance, regular mailings sent to physicians by pharmaceutical companies are as controlled as publications, without having the readership request the mailings—at first. But very specialized mailers often offer free newsletters, which usually have to be requested. The line between controlled print circulation and controlled direct mail begins to blur here, especially when the free newsletters are elaborately printed publications, often with house ads. Controlled direct mail circulation often becomes another medium: card decks. These cooperative mailings of business reply cards with promotional messages sent to a particular targeted market (accountants, investors, gardeners) usually deliver very low response rates, but they offer smaller mailers an inexpensive opportunity to sell to markets they otherwise couldn't afford to reach.

• *Bulk circulation.* Often used to reach all the employees of large organizations. Arrangements are made with the office manager or personnel manager to distribute, along with the morning's mail, copies of a direct mail package with particular interest to the organization: book catalogs, fund-raising appeals, insurance programs, discounted items, or special offers from local merchants. Just before school opening, teachers' mailboxes are stuffed with bulk-delivered mail. Occupant mailings, which are broadcast to everybody at a particular address, are usually used to deliver samples and coupons. However, two of the key assets of direct mail—personalization and keyed responses—are lost in this method of delivery. Obviously, bulk circulation is an area where the lines between direct mail and sales promotion begin to blur.

• *Pass-along circulation.* Not used as often in direct mail as it might be. Publishers estimate that one copy of a magazine can be read by as many as five people. The appeal of a direct mail letter is limited to the addressee, but there are ways of extending that reach. For instance, in a health promotion, enclose another copy of the letter for the spouse. In a business-to-business package, have another copy of the letter enclosed for a colleague or the chief financial officer, or for distribution to the board of directors, or to the firm's accountant or banker. In the case of a successful mailing, answer with an acknowledgment and a copy of the previous letter, which the customer is invited to pass along to a friend.

Two-Step Mailings: Double Trouble or Twice as Effective?

Direct mail is considered one advertising medium that is free from the tyranny of time. The deadlines you have to meet are of your own making. No publisher or broadcaster forces you to schedule everything according to his requirements.

Of course, this isn't so. Direct mail is subject to deadlines set by other people, including mailing houses, list suppliers, lettershops, and printers. Their deadlines are not as rigorous as print and broadcast media, but nevertheless, if you want to get into the mail by a certain date, you had better work around the schedule they give you.

Perhaps marching to the beat of others has made direct mailers a little hesitant about two-step mailings. These mailings work in tandem. A short time after the initial drop, another mailing, a duplicate of the first, is sent to the same list.

It calls for, if not exactly split-second timing, a sense of rhythm and judgment about how to space the two mailings. Besides another set of deadlines and schedules to meet, problems of overkill and overbudget can arise. And list owners often hesitate before allowing their lists to be hit with a one-two punch this way.

Then why go through this duplicating exercise at all? Will double the trouble bring you double the response? Not really. If successful, you might find yourself with a 15 or 20 percent increase in response at most.

It's really an attempt to achieve cumulative recognition. If the target evaded you the first time out, perhaps it will slow down long enough the second time to recognize the mailing and sit down and read it. A two-step mailing differs from the standard letter series, where a number of packages may be sent to the same person over a period of time, each package selling a different feature, emphasizing another benefit, or using different offers. A two-step is the *same* promotion without change. And it differs from the standard repeat mailings to the same list over six months or a year by telescoping the time period.

Mailing No. 2 can also serve as a big P.S., in those instances where the first mailing may have been read and not acted on. Direct mailers, incurable optimists and pessimists at the same time, may object that the second mailing will poison the waters, and that the prospects will cancel the original order. The chances are good that, if they do react at all, it may be to return the second order form with a scrawled "have already ordered this." If you have done your homework well and have located the most logical potential customers, you can feel sure they won't be upset at the thought of two mailings from the same source. You can suggest that they pass the message on to a friend or neighbor. And if your fulfillment procedures are good, you may be able to stop mailing No. 2 from going out to people who have already answered you.

A variation on this type of mailing is the simultaneous release of two mailings on the same day to the same list. It may be the same mailing, or you may use a control and a test package—and hope that both reach the prospect at the same time.

There's still a third variation: the support mailing. Traditionally, support advertising is done through another medium. A TV spot reminds people to look in their mailboxes for a sweepstakes offer. Or an ad repeats a TV message. Or a telephone call follows up a mailing. When done through direct mail alone, it's usually in the form of a postcard or brief note preceding the main package by a week or two. (An American Express Optima credit card promotion to American Express Gold Card members used this device.)

A subtle if ambitious variation is to have both support and main mailing reach the prospect at the same time. The postcard, for instance, draws attention to the spectacular package. This is a risky technique, because again you have to hope that both items are delivered on the same day, the chances of which are roughly those of your winning the Publishers Clearing House sweeps.

To cut those odds down a bit, an extravagant solution is to mail the spectacular package by overnight carrier and send the support message via mailgram. But this is recommended only if you're selling very large diamonds or very small islands to a choice number of people who you judge will be receptive to this sort of promotional blitzkrieg.

In most cases, a specialized product for a specialized audience doesn't warrant this kind of effort or expense, which can even be counterproductive. Support and cumulative promotions do have a place when you're competing for attention in heavily used media, especially if you're offering a general product or service to a broad audience. They can be effective reminders that, by simply and quickly following up on the original sales call, can create their own selling opportunities.

CHAPTER 5

Promoting Financial Services Through Direct Marketing

Technology Transforms Financial Services

Writing in the July–August 1960 *Harvard Business Review*, Theodore Levitt showed how the railroads lost out to automobiles and airplanes. His seminal article "Marketing Myopia" noted that railroad owners believed that they were in the train business, rather than the transportation industry. Product-oriented rather than consumer-oriented, they were ready to be dealt a death blow by nontraditional competitors.

In contrast, Walter Wriston, former chairman of CitiCorp, made it perfectly clear that his bank was in the communications business, not banking. CitiCorp operates *two* competing electronic stock-reporting services, Quotron and StreetSense. And it has offered retail customers the chance to do their bank business at home, via computer. Chemical Bank, the giant New York financial institution, also offers customers the ability to get an update on their balance and pay bills via computer.

A fast-growing electronic technology means that banks can sell their services and execute transactions on a one-to-one basis. Computer terminals and TV sets have opened a new era for bank direct marketing.

This give-and-take does more than offer convenience to customers. It also improves the banking direct marketer's ability to segment market and message. Its precise audience targeting and instant order fulfillment virtually put a bank branch into every home, cutting across old geographical limitations and changing the very concept of banking from a staid, tradition-bound business to a contemporary, no-holds-barred service.

Another electronic pipeline also has potential direct marketing application: the computerized investing information service. Dow Jones, Standard & Poor's, and CitiBank offer huge files of financial information to investors, brokers, and investment managers, with vital statistical and advisory information transmitted immediately to a user's desk or to a hand-held wireless receiver.

The opportunity for *marketing* brokerage and other financial services is there, an idea whose time has come. The Source and Compuserve, national computer networks, offer subscribers a communications service, a bulletin board, computer conference call convenience, airline schedules and booking, and electronic shopping as well as brokerage services.

Ultrasophisticated satellite transmission of TV programs allows reception by personal satellite dish. The direct marketer can thereby pinpoint audiences in a small geographical area—the territory served by a single branch of a bank, for instance. Informative commercials can be changed to reflect local conditions: seasonality, events, weather. Neighbors can be featured and local landmarks shown.

By building up an accurate profile of people's spending and investing habits and tracking their consumer behavior, direct marketers can accurately segment those portions of the population most likely to buy the most profitable services. Through strategic segmentation and electronic technology, financial services can be sold on a much more cost-effective basis.

Direct marketing should be used by financial service institutions to determine what markets they ought to service, what financial products the consumer is likely to want, and even what fees to charge.

Instant communication and electronic payment systems spell opportunity for financial institutions willing to market their products on a carefully segmented basis.

How to Manage Financial Direct Marketing

A sure sign of the growing sophistication of financial marketing is the new importance of the direct marketing manager. As financial organizations change their identity and new and diversified products and services have to be sold in a very competitive environment, the direct marketing manager's role has changed from expediter of sales letters to full marketing partner.

Whether working in a bank, a brokerage house, an insurance company, a mutual-fund house, or a financial supermarket, today's direct marketing manager has new job qualifications.

• *A thorough comprehension of the product or service and its marketability through direct response techniques.* This includes a knowledge of government and industry compliance regulations and an understanding of the financial organization's own procedures for approving copy. (Many a brilliant package has been launched only to be shipwrecked on the reefs of a bank or broker's own legal department's refusal to approve the mailing.)

• *An ability to organize a thorough marketing plan.* This includes a talent for selling the strategy to management through presentation, argumentation, behind-the-scenes maneuvering, and some refined arm twisting. To be complete, the plan has to include scenarios and "what-if" options, with contingency budgets carefully sprinkled throughout. And it has to be realistic. An overly optimistic marketing plan, based on a misread response, could poison the waters for similar projects for years ahead. On the other hand, a purely defensive pessimism is unfair to the direct marketing unit, the product, and the good sense of management. A series of superlative and surprising successes will raise questions about the manager's predictive abilities. (In financial marketing, nothing succeeds like success, but nothing fails like undue success.) Inadequate fulfillment, undertrained personnel, disappointed customers, and overtaxed departments will require a lot of explaining on the part of the direct marketing manager. "No surprises" is the rule.

• *An ability to orchestrate the effort.* Besides the responsibility for the direct marketing department, the direct marketing manager has to assemble and direct the other players: the bank officials, who have to have the answers for customers bringing in a sales letter; the service center or fulfillment house, which needs followup material already inventoried and ready to be mailed; the advertising and sales promotion specialists supplying branch offices; the sales manager and sales personnel, who need carefully written telephone routines (approved by legal staff before use).

• *A gift for sparking good concepts and ideas.* Advertising agencies are important marketing partners, but a good direct marketing manager has to have complete familiarity with the product and service, the market, and the financial organization's operations. Should the next mailing be a computerized jumbo package? Or should it be a simple letter and reply form? Should the couponed ad offer a premium or not? Before creative people can answer these questions, the direct marketing manager must weigh alternatives, supply direction, offer suggestions, and veto unworkable concepts.

The good direct marketing manager is also alert to changes in the marketplace, can see the subtleties in results, and has a good idea of the competition's strategies. By gathering intelligence on developments in his organization, the industry, and even the regulatory agencies, he or she can filter out the meaningless and home in on the facts that can turn a tepid mailing into a resounding success. A good direct marketing manager can also resist the temptation to become a spokesperson for management, reading the minds of the inhabitants of the executive suite instead of concentrating on the needs of the consumer.

Sometimes confused with an advertising manager or sales promotion director, the direct marketing manager of a financial institution has a stronger role than either. Using skills tempered in the tough arena of response-oriented marketing, the direct marketing manager has a major responsibility in today's financial organization, as competition increases, as services and products multiply, and as consumers shy away from once-popular investments, question promotions, and shop more more carefully than in the past.

How to Make the Best Use of Form Letters in Financial Direct Marketing

Letters of *dis*credit may be one of the biggest complaints of bank and brokerage customers who receive an old-fashioned, often frighteningly unclear, form letter in answer to a simple request. The best efforts of direct marketers in banking and other financial services can be canceled by these turgid, sometimes tactless followup or fulfillment letters, which, in too many instances, were conceived years ago by lawyers, accountants, sales or office managers, or pension managers, rather than direct marketing specialists.

Of course, the use of standard letters is a hallowed tradition that goes back to ancient Greece and Rome. In fact, the ancestor of all direct mail writers was probably Demetrius Phalereus (*c.* 345–283 B.C.), credited with the first compilation of guide letters for all occasions, public and private.

In modern business practice, three kinds of standard letters may be found: (1) preprinted or computerized form letters, which can range from cover letters to emendations of contracts and usually have space for amounts, dates, and reference numbers; (2) letter forms—those insulting pseudo-epistles—notices, announcements or statement stuffers—that start off with a deflating, anonymous "Dear Customer" and usually remind readers that missing credit cards should be promptly reported; and (3) guide letters, standardized letter formats developed for the guidance of letter writers. They are found in manuals or looseleaf binders, indexed so that the uninspired correspondent (or harried sales manager) need only look up a subject and use the suggested text for a personalized response. Conservative organizations usually lock the writer into a prescribed format, with punctuation, indentation, and salutation strictly set down. More daring firms offer a basic text, with several alternative paragraphs, allowing the writer to choose from column A and column B.

Good standard letters are office workhorses. They can save time, achieve results, and free both correspondent and recipient from pointless personal meetings or phone conversations. Deadlines, ticklish problems, and elusive phraseology are headaches that good business-letter models can cure. They often represent a consensus of opinion from among the best minds in the organization, with the legal department's stamp of approval. These letters will always be useful as sources of ideas. But if the letters are ill formed, formless, or uninformative, all this productivity will be nullified.

The problem usually lies with the original writer. It's not often that these letters are written by direct marketers. Instead, executives in personnel, credit, data processing, legal, or sales, and branch, loan, mortgage, or trust officers devise solutions to their specific correspondence problems of the moment. Then the letters become part of office routine, never to be questioned or scrutinized.

Putting Life Into Form Letters

The direct marketer's first task is to *demand* a review of these standard letters, and then eliminate cant, turning letter forms into real printed pieces and converting pointless formality into working documents. At first, the job may seem overwhelming. For the collector of infamous form letters, it's almost like being attacked by a flock of rare and dangerous birds.

THE BIRD-WATCHER'S GUIDE

Take the "raucous rude-runner." Usually hatched by a bank, its cry is a shrill, tactless one-liner: "Your application for a loan has not been approved." No reason given. No attempt to soften the blow. No suggestions offered on how to resubmit a loan application. And millions of dollars spent in advertising go down the drain as still another prospect is treated like a suspect.

Its cousin, the "razor-billed rejector," is found in the mail of unsuccessful job applicants. Drab and unassuming, it is a photocopied note initialed by a secretary, telling the applicant that she didn't get the job. Period. Again, no reason. No wishes for success elsewhere. Reading the note, the brooding applicant may blame the personnel manager's politics, the bank's policy, or the phases of the moon. Any reason will do, since no reason was tendered. The eggs laid by this particular bird may hatch years later when the unsuccessful job applicant has the opportunity to slander the bank, ignore its bid for business, or take her company's business elsewhere.

The "lesser catch-all," an unsuccessful predator that attempts to lure its prey with a gift, is usually found around life insurance agencies. This preprinted letter offers to exchange a pocket dictionary or some other cheap premium for one's birth date, obviously an attempt to seize the subject's soul. A subspecies frequents local branches of banks, where it halfheartedly offers a free gift to visitors. Sometimes, the customer's name may be scrawled on the top of the letter, usually by the shanghaied teenage offspring of the prospecting salesperson. This form letter appears to be dying out—of starvation, no doubt.

The "flint-eyed harrier" is a carrion eater. Able to sense a failing victim from miles away, it swoops down on a delinquent mortgage player or borrower, crying: "The matter has been referred to our attorneys." Its nest is feathered by thousands of repossessions and garnishees.

Other birds of this feather include the "hurt pouter" ("You haven't used your credit card in a long, long time"), the "account churner" ("Here's a nice little stock we're recommending"), the "co-maker fault finder" ("As the co-signer, you're responsible for paying the balance in full at once"), and the "foreclosing house snapper" ("It will be necessary to initiate foreclosure").

Sadly, much of this thoughtless mail is generated by otherwise thoughtful and conscientious people who would never write such things on their own. But they must go by the book, and in this case the book of standard letter forms or suggested models is Holy Writ.

THE DEPARTMENTAL REVIEW

The remedy? The direct marketer should ask each department to send its manual of standard letters for review. Keep an eye out for problems in the following areas:

1. *Credit and collection.* Are the letters violating any recent federal or state laws? Are they effective? Are they capable of alienating customers? Are they comprehensible? Do they sound like Lord Byron's creditor-tailor, "crawling on his knees while shaking his fist"?

2. *Mortgage loans.* Instead of preprinted forms, a personal letter that is warm and friendly can generate prompt payment, and will stimulate goodwill rather than make unpalatable a relationship that must continue for many years.

3. *Complaints and adjustments.* Mass-produced form letters or checkoff notes give the impression that your organization is engulfed by problems. Treat each complaint or adjustment as a unique or rare occurrence. Computer programs allow you to turn out individually typed and addressed form letters.

4. *Trusts and estates.* Standard letters in this area should be flexible enough to allow for any of the unique situations encountered in trusts, estates, and investments. One customer has to know what a trust account is; another has to be told what an executor does; and a third has to be reassured about the confidentiality of trust agreements. Using a cold, formal, lifeless letter written a generation ago reflects poorly on the personal nature of a trust department.

THE FORM-LETTER AUDIT

As you begin your review of these letters, ask these six questions of each one.

1. *Is the letter free from jargon?* The old-fashioned prose once so common in financial correspondence has now largely disappeared—replaced by an inhuman jargon. "Yours of the fourth ult" has now given place to "preprocessing of your application has now been effected." Of course, some legal language cannot be avoided, and all letters should be cleared with the legal department as a matter of routine. Be prepared to fight for simplicity and clarity, but remember that rules of libel, contract, and consumer rights need to be observed and policed.

2. *Is the letter likely to be read?* Don't begin a letter with a participle. It tells readers that this letter is dull. Instead, get their attention and interest by telling them at once what you are going to do for them.

3. *Will the letter make a friend?* Give the reader the good news first. By accentuating the positive, you can make it easier when you tell him you're foreclosing his house.

4. *Are you informative?* Let the reader behind the scenes. Tell him something about the bond aftermarket, how a finance charge is computed, why his checks keep bouncing.

5. *Are you polite?* Honey will always get you more than vinegar. Tact and courtesy will be remembered and reciprocated. Caution: Don't be overfriendly. A lighthearted quip has no place in a financial discussion. You're talking about somebody's money, and that's serious!

6. *Have you asked for action?* Make it easy for recipients to do what you ask them to do. Tell them to phone—and give them the phone number in the body of the letter, even if it's printed on top. Enclose a business reply envelope for their answer. Spell out the actions you want them to take.

It's good practice to check out your organization's standard letters at frequent intervals. They may have been carefully designed to solve problems at the time by the best minds available, but times change. And while standard letters do have their place in repetitive situations, and a carefully prepared letter is better than one written on the spur of the moment, no letter should ever be routine. It's simply . . . bad form.

A Surefire Mailing List for Banks

Are you in bank direct marketing? I know someone who is your ideal prospect for bank services. She's affluent, lives and works in the territory served by your bank, already knows quite a lot about your bank, and appreciates your bank's need to show a profit.

This paragon of bankability needs more than just a checking or savings account; she is also an eager candidate for personal banking, investment, and trust services. She looks forward to receiving and using all the plastic cards your bank can bestow on her, and is joyful at the prospect of opening a money market account. She also wants to hear from management, and even now reads your bank's ads with great interest. All she needs from you is an invitation, so she can proceed to do business with your bank.

If you were offered a mailing list of people fitting this profile, you'd kill for it, wouldn't you? At the very least, you'd be happy to pay a premium for its one-time use.

Good news: For many banks, this list is already available, and you can use it as often as you wish. In fact it's yours—free of charge. And once a year, your bank actually does use it, but then lays it to rest for another year.

Just check with your investor relations department, because the list we're talking about contains the names of your bank's *shareholders*. The list may (or may not) be quite small, but it's very hot— even though the annual statement may be the only regular mailing it gets from your bank. All you have to do is to tap the reservoir of intangible goodwill that exists between bank and shareholder.

Before mailing to this list, you will want to put it through the usual screens, of course. Owning bank shares doesn't automatically make a person a good credit risk, for instance. And many shares are owned by out-of-towners or institutions, and in the names of brokerage houses.

But filtering out these unwanted names still yields a substantial assemblage of prospects who have not been tapped as frequently as you might expect. *In fact, bank shareholders do not necessarily do business with the bank whose shares they own—mainly because they've never been asked.*

Not all banks are eager to mail to their shareholders. Some may feel that shareholders shouldn't be "bothered," citing the parable of the sleeping tiger. Others may be reluctant to let shareholders know just how their dividends are earned. ("You mean that the bank actually sells health and accident insurance to its credit-card holders?") And others may think that affluent shareholders may not want to do business with, say, a small neighborhood bank.

But shareholders today don't live in ivory towers. And in the same way that an advertising agency may encourage its employees to use the products of its clients, shareholders should be encouraged to use the services of the bank whose shares pay them dividends. Bonus: Shareholders who are up-to-date with management's way of doing business, if it is presented correctly, are apt to be staunch friends at proxy time.

Odds are, shareholders who are given half a chance to do business with the bank they "own" will be more than ready to sign up for everything from a savings account (fueled with bank dividends) to a safe deposit box where their bank stock certificates can rest securely.

Important: Once shareholders start to receive mail from their bank, they will want to remain on your mailing list. And they can get quite vocal at annual shareholder meetings, if they're cut off. In fact, they have been known to go right to the CEO if they've been dropped from mailings; one reason, perhaps, why management may be reluctant to mail to them in the first place.

How large a list does a bank usually possess? While a small bank may count its individual shareholders in hundreds, and a very small bank in scores or dozens, the large bank may have thousands of names to mail to.

If you have access to the bank's shareholder list, you own a mailing list of people clamoring for your direct mail, a free list where you'll find the names of some of your hottest prospects. It would be a shame not to mail to them whenever you want to reach the ideal customer.

Mining Your Shareholder List With These Twenty-Eight Often Overlooked Promotions

1. Get referrals for new business.
2. Keep shareholders up-to-date with management activities by sending them copies of press releases. (Avoid "insider divulgence" problems by mailing to shareholders *after* mailing to the press.)
3. Send advance copies of newspaper and magazine ads.
4. Invite shareholders to advance screenings of TV commercials.
5. Test new services by introducing them to shareholders before announcing them to the public.
6. Explain changes in services and policies. Break news of branch closings, elimination of services, or fee increases to stockholders first, to enlist their support.
7. Survey for complaints, ideas, and suggestions.
8. Offer multiple services—personal banking and business payroll, for instance.
9. Enclose savings or checking account applications with bank dividend checks if your bank handles its own dividend payments.
10. Win back inactive customers who are also shareholders with a "personal" letter from the CEO.
11. Develop special offers just for shareholders.
12. Sell unusual services to shareholders, like a distinctive kind of check.
13. Enlist shareholder support in community activities that the bank is participating in.
14. Counter rumors of bank troubles and build confidence in the bank.
15. Promote new branch offerings.
16. Mail a newsletter on a regular basis, like First National Bank of Dallas's "Stockholders' News Release."

17. Sponsor a special anniversary promotion with an after-hours open house. When First National Bank of Lebanon, Pennsylvania, celebrated its centennial, 500 shareholders were mailed personal invitations to the bank's open house.
18. Promote account transfers from other banks. Provide personalized forms to make the transfer as easy as possible.
19. Keep shareholders informed of personnel changes, especially in their neighborhood branches.
20. Promote international services, including introductions to overseas correspondents, letters of credit, and travelers' checks.
21. Offer the free use of your bank's financial research library.
22. Segregate bank statements of shareholders who happen to be customers and mail with a personal note from management.
23. Waive fees for overdrafts.
24. Offer office space in the bank.
25. Hold seminars on banking, with updates on upcoming rules and regulations that can affect your bank and shareholders' dividends.
26. Assign a personal banker to shareholders.
27. Offer special parking privileges.
28. Promote third-party referrals, by encouraging shareholders to promote bank services among their lawyers, accountants, and tax advisers.

Mailing to a shareholder list is like getting an extra ride on a mailing for very little extra. You'll find that, whether it's a specially targeted mailing or a broadscale effort, direct marketing to a bank's shareholders can pay off with extra interest.

CHAPTER 6

Brainstorming Tips for Better Ideas

Investing in Ideas Can Pay Big Dividends

Creativity is an asset you won't find on a balance sheet, but it can mean the difference between profit and loss in a direct marketing operation.

Perhaps one way of defining creativity is to call it *the process of achieving novelty*. How to sell a similar product or service in a different way. How to make one company stand out from all the rest. How to position. How to find a unique selling proposition. How to isolate the best offer. How to introduce a new product or create a new service. How to put old wine in new bottles. How to rewin friends and rewoo the alienated.

Obviously, creativity in marketing can't be compared to the

inspiration, illumination, or intuition achieved in splendid isolation in one's own sweet time. The real world intrudes. Opportunities hover. Deadlines loom. Clients demand. Crises impend. Competitors encroach. Other projects impinge. You're under the gun to come up with a new package or a new ad or new script in days— maybe hours. And to do it again and again.

Mozart, Michelangelo, or Einstein aside, the kind of dependable, instant creativity often needed in direct marketing can actually be stimulated through certain techniques now available to any individual—the buttoned-down number cruncher as well as the so-called ideator. Thanks to new discoveries in psychology, effective educational procedures have evolved that can teach any person to be creative. Blocked copywriters or art directors can be helped to quickly overcome their problems without costly analysis or painful soul searching. These approaches include role playing, lateral thinking, cognitive procedures, programmed methods, brainstorming, synectics, and personality-insight techniques.

Here are some of the ideas currently being used by direct marketing people today. These methods are useful in facilitating innovative thinking, and they should be part of any direct marketing person's arsenal of creative weapons.

REDEFINITION

A method many have found particularly useful is redefinition, which increases the range of possible ideas available. Just step back and take a new look at a product, service, benefit, or offer. By giving it a new name, you give it a whole new identity and personality and set of characteristics, characteristics previously overlooked.

I was once faced with the horrible prospect of trying to beat a control created three decades earlier by the great Vic Schwab himself. Victor O. Schwab was one of the pioneers of mail order advertising, and his advertising agency's ads for the Book-of-the-Month Club and Charles Atlas, for instance, had been instrumental in building great enterprises from coupons.

Anyway, the Master had once written an ad for the Classics Club, a book club selling books by famous philosophers, orators, statesmen, et al. It was a handy way to collect, and someday read, books by Aristotle, Plato, and other great thinkers of Western civilization.

The headline of the control ad simply offered three books for $1 as an introduction to the club. And nothing had ever come close to beating it. But now it was getting tired. Would I take a stab at it?

Three books were offered, works by Plato, Aristotle, and Marcus Aurelius. To the public these books were dry as dust. Heavy going. Dated and irrelevant.

There were many copy options open to me. I could extol the utility of these books. The excitement within their pages. Their influence. The "heritage" approach (own a piece of Western civilization). The coffee-table book strategy. But each had been tried and found wanting.

I hefted these books. Why call them books at all?

The prospective members of the Classics Club weren't particularly intellectual. We had to get them excited. Books per se were not interesting. They meant work. You had to, well, read them.

So I redefined the product. I created the books afresh—this time as individuals. Sages, geniuses, teachers. In the headline I asked the reader to "Let These Three Wise Men into Your Home. Later, You Might Like to Invite Their Friends." Body text used every benefit in my quiver from "helping you think more clearly" to "giving the kids a boost in school." All sweet and reasonable, as Len Reiss, the direct marketing mentor for an entire generation of copywriters, later said.

The approach was effective. The new ad unseated Vic Schwab's control. In an article in *Advertising Age*, the well-known Chicago ad man Jim Kobs called it the ad he wished he had written. And many years later, the ad is still running.

HYPOTHESIS

This approach comes from Tom Collins, a founder of Rapp & Collins, the New York advertising agency. To develop new space ads, Collins, who studied under Vic Schwab, would create a series of "what-if concepts"—hypotheses about the prospect, price, offer, product, or benefits. Then, according to Jim Kobs's book *Profitable*

Direct Marketing (Crain Books, 1979), Collins would build a separate ad around each hypothesis.

For example, a control ad for a music home-study course showed a woman playing the piano. But Collins argued that today a teenager playing the guitar may be a better prospect. This hypothesis was tested. And won. The hypothesis approach can be particularly effective when building a campaign, because each element in an ad can be expanded into a hypothesis for an ad of its own.

ADDING AND EXTRACTING

As reported in Robert Stone's book *Successful Direct Marketing Methods* (Crain Books, 1975), copywriter Sol Blumenfeld's strategy for idea generation includes the additive approach. Try to add something to every control package that will increase its efficiency without adding much to the cost; for example, a buck slip (lift letter). Or consider adding an involvement device such as a token or stamp to the order form.

Another Blumenfeld tactic is the extractive approach—a blessing when you have a deadline. Review the control package or current ad and pull a potential winner out of some line buried in body copy, by turning it into the headline or theme of a new effort.

Direct marketing success calls for a stream of concepts and innovations. As a cost-effective, cost-responsible medium, direct marketing doesn't have a muse and we can't afford to wait for inspiration. Which is why, as Ed Nash noted in his *Direct Marketing: Strategy/Planning/Execution* (McGraw-Hill, 1982), structured creativity is emerging as a force in direct marketing.

How Direct Mail Can Borrow From Radio

The medium of radio is becoming popular again as an advertising vehicle for direct response. For the writers, it's a two-way street: Direct mail writers take to radio commercials eagerly, and broadcast writers can bring their special skills to direct mail, giving it an interesting flavor. There are at least three devices from radio that can be of service in direct mail.

BREVITY

The first is the necessity to be brief. You just can't run on in radio. If the commercial is thirty seconds long, you can't write thirty-two seconds' worth of copy. So a copywriter learns that you don't have to repeat anything to make a point. That you can sell with inference and tone and pacing. That simple words work better than complicated ones. And that brief sentences are easily comprehended, while long, involved sentences can baffle the listener.

Transferring these lessons to direct mail can transmute a dull package into a golden moneymaker. For instance, very long copy is sometimes necessary to sell something. But if the copy is long only because it reiterates the same points, you're wasting your time and your reader's. Writing broadcast copy can teach you how to sell gracefully and quickly. In this impatient era, when most people just don't have time to read a lot of words, stylish brevity can win you friends and customers.

CONTIGUITY

Another selling concept you might want to borrow from radio is contiguity. This describes two programs next to each other in time and sequence that are not interrupted for commercials or announcements.

A mailer who has two products might drop two mailings to the same household at the same time. For instance, a magazine publisher offering a photography magazine and a travel magazine might send separate but equal packages to the same list. Each package would identify the publisher, but would not refer to the other offer, so as not to detract from the subject of the mailing. (This can be tested, of course.)

Assuming the list has potential for the two magazines, synergy might create a harder-selling environment, with both publications benefiting. (Some observers will quietly point out that two different mailings from the same publisher to the same list at the same time might confuse recipients, and make them decide to accept no offer at all. That's why a test is so important.)

HITCHHIKING

The third radio device is hitchhiking. This is a short commercial near the end of a sponsored program, which pushes a product not previously mentioned. This "by-the-way, folks" reminder is a way of giving exposure to a small-budget product, taking advantage of any halo effect emitted by the heavily advertised item.

In a mail package, some other product can hitch a ride with a postscript, buck slip, flier, or an additional checkoff on the order form. This is a way to introduce a product on the cheap or to sell off excess inventory. Because direct mail can be more accurately focused than radio, only a portion of a mailing need receive this hitchhiker. So you can test it without totally committing yourself, or send it to only those names you judge to have the greatest interest in the offer. It's a way of getting the hitchhiker to pay the tolls.

Direct marketers have found that it's essential to be able to move in and out of different media to take advantage of different windows of opportunity. The successful copywriter doesn't have to put on another hat to work in a different medium, though. The lessons learned on one platform can be applied at another time in another place, often with gratifying results.

Break the Copy Rules and Make It Pay

The unquestioning acceptance of rules can lead to dullness and slackness. Nowhere is this more true than in direct marketing copy, where generations of very successful practitioners have laid down a body of rules for their less successful successors to follow.

Fortunately, more sophisticated marketing techniques and computerized production facilities have led today's direct marketing practitioners to question many of yesterday's principles. I say *fortunately*, because competition for attention and sales has never been stronger, and new tactics and strategies are called for. Take a new look at these treasured laws, which are now beginning to show their age.

1. *Avoid the personal pronoun.* Some mighty contorted copy has been written in order to observe this rule. While probably nobody is interested in an entire letter devoted to the problems of the writer, you have to remember that natural speech uses *I* a lot more than *you.* You're not being selfish or bragging if you refer to yourself.

Indeed, if you assault the reader with *you* wherever possible, you may end up sounding hectoring, dogmatic, and impersonal. Your ad may sound like a drill instructor's litany of commands. Your letter may give the unfortunate effect of a legal writ.

Try to strike a balance between the second-person singular and the first-person pronoun, and you will create a warm personality who sincerely cares about the reader.

2. *Ask for the order.* Good advice, but let's qualify it. Give the prospect a good reason for becoming a customer. Why close a letter or ad with a simple-minded bid for action when you can help readers make up their mind?

Some effective reasons for sending in the coupon or mailing back the order form or phoning the 800 number can be: beating a deadline, a gift for early-bird orders, limited quantities available, the danger of losing out to your competitors, or "early rot"—the offer is at its peak of ripeness right now and to wait is to lose its freshness or strength.

3. *Sell the sizzle, not the steak.* Fine, if you're selling barbecue pits. This rule from the golden days of salesmanship presumed that the consumer was an easily swayed sucker who could be sold anything by a golden-tongued "drummer."

It's been the downfall of many good salespeople who assiduously practiced the art of baloney making while ignoring, to their peril, the innards of the product or service they were offering. The sizzle *comes from* the steak and can't be treated separately.

Know your product or service, and you'll land squarely on the basic reason why somebody should buy it. Share the knowledge in your promotion by telling as well as selling, and you will have made a sale the easy way, without burning your fingers with the sizzle.

4. *Your present customers are your best ones.* This maxim is often used when justifying a mailing to your current customer base. It makes excellent sense, but it doesn't go far enough. Your present customer is also fair game for your *competitor.* By taking your present customers for granted, you may be giving up turf to the other team.

What you ought to consider in any mailing to your customers are the reasons that brought them into the fold in the first place. Was it the chance to save money? A special offer? A referral? Your reputation for service? Convenience? A trial offer?

When you do a mailing that includes current customers, don't ignore their special nature. For instance, your letters may be more personal than those addressed to an outside list. You may want to resell them on your product or service, to strengthen the confidence they have in you. And you may want to offer some additional inducement for action (while carefully factoring in these elements when analyzing results, of course.)

5. *Insist on your prospects* printing *their name and address.* The ad could be a beautiful articulation of reasons and benefits to buy a product, with every word carefully measured to evoke good feelings, but then the coupon summarily commands you to "please print."

"Ah," you say, "but it's so simple to print a name and address, and it can save our fulfillment people a lot of time and prevent a lot of errors."

Yes, but many people are offended by the suggestion that their handwriting is awful, and you're giving them an excuse for not replying. So, if you have the opportunity, test coupons with the "please print" versus no request and see if it does make a difference.

Suggestions have a way of ossifying into rules. These ideas aren't chiseled in stone, and neither are the rules we've inherited in direct marketing. Not all rules need to be broken, but you can go out and bend them a little every now and then.

Fifteen Paths to Productive and Creative Meetings

When a meeting is structured and handled correctly, it can contribute to the creative effort as much as the time spent staring at a drawing board or computer screen or sheet of typing paper.

To succeed, a structured meeting usually needs a defined task or goal and a controlled process under the supervision of a leader. A successful meeting can also be a group-centered discussion, designed to fulfill needs of an individual or group, such as studying, learning, or complaining. So long as the purpose of the meeting is defined and certain rules applied, it becomes relatively easy to keep it on track.

There are some fifteen different kinds of meetings. For your next get-together—inter- and intradepartmental, group, client-agency, buyer-vendor, corporate, or industry—you may want to consider one or more from this "shopping list."

1. *Lecture.* For one-way communication. A qualified person delivers a carefully prepared oral presentation of a subject. No audience participation.

2. *Forum.* For minimal two-way communciation. A person delivers a speech and a moderator chairs an open discussion immediately afterward. A good learning method.

3. *Panel.* Assign from three to six persons to a topic for discussion. The panel members should have an interest and competence in the subject and proven ability to speak in front of a group. A moderator usually prepares questions in advance to keep the discussion going.

4. *Panel-forum.* Same as a panel, with one addition: an audience-participation period. The moderator fields questions from the audience, often collecting the questions before the panel discussion. A good meeting structure when both audience and panelists are more or less peers; for instance, at a copy club.

5. *Symposium.* Several people each speak on different aspects of the same topic or on closely related topics. Usually chaired by a moderator. A good way to present technological changes in printing or list management, for instance.

6. *Symposium-forum.* A symposium followed by an audience discussion period. The moderator should have skills in handling an

audience and stimulating group participation. Could be deadly when moderator, through ignorance of each speaker's special expertise, can't direct questions. Or when the moderator can't cut short a windy dissertation from somebody in the audience.

7. *Colloquy.* Ideal with large audiences. A group of panelists are interviewed by several representatives of the audience, who ask questions and raise issues to be dealt with by the panelists. Good for national meetings of sales organizations or large companies faced with new developments—increasing competition, new management, or a scandal. Versions of the colloquy may be found in televised discussions on Sunday morning, where several journalists, representing a media pool, will question several experts, or at the presidential debates, where candidates are questioned by reporters.

8. *Group discussion.* One of the most important types of structured meetings in direct marketing. As many as twenty participants talk about a topic of shared interest, guided by a trained leader. Each participant is given the opportunity to share ideas or experiences with the others. An excellent way to train newcomers, reveal areas of stress, and focus on a particular problem. Used by some organizations to launch the creation of a direct marketing effort, and later to dissect results. Not all participants need be writers or art directors or even have a role in the particular effort; they should, however, be able to share their knowledge or special expertise with others.

9. *Conference.* A good way to gather information and discuss a mutual problem. A reasonable solution is desirable, but the goal can be as simple as identifying the problem. Ideal for improving vendor-customer relations.

10. *Convention.* An assembly of participants who represent local units or organizations. Uses panels, forums, speeches, group discussions to explore and act on various problems. A communications medium that calls for careful planning, production, and direction.

11. *Committee.* When the entire group can't handle a task efficiently, a small group of individuals may be assigned the job. A committee may study a particular problem, reach a conclusion, and, if so authorized, act. The committee usually prepares a report as its final task. In large organizations, it may be called a task force or ad hoc group. A good way to get several able individuals or several groups working on the same problem.

12. *Seminar.* An expert or specialist guides a group of people in the study of a subject. The usual procedure is to identify the problem and explore it, discuss or design the research needed to solve it, conduct the research, share the findings with the group, and reach a conclusion on the basis of the research. With sociology and computers now vital tools of list management, and state and local laws affecting direct marketing more directly, seminars will assume greater importance in the ongoing education of direct marketing practitioners.

13. *Institute.* This is a series of meetings for a group of people who come together in a planned and organized manner to learn about a special problem or field. The series may be for a day or two or may continue for years. Authorities present an organized body of knowledge to the learners, who usually work in groups with perhaps some individual study. Often the goal of the institute is to train participants to pass on knowledge to others. In direct marketing it can be used to deliver instruction in or information about advanced techniques—media selection, production, creativity, management. The institute itself can be a product or service to be marketed, either alone or in connection with another product or service. For instance, a trade magazine may sponsor an institute in its special area of expertise, to be packaged and sold by direct marketing. A certificate or diploma might be issued at the end of an institute.

14. *Clinic.* An excellent way to meet certain problems head on. If a catalog is not achieving its sales goal, for instance, or a fund raiser is encountering resistance to a new campaign, or new products are having difficulty being launched, this structured meeting can establish a way to solve the specific problem. Devices used may

include case studies, demonstrations, field trips, and shared experiences.

15. *Workshop*. The workshop is a group of people with a common interest or problem who meet for an extended period of time. Their goal: to improve their individual proficiency and ability through study, research, and discussion. This is an opportunity that very large organizations and advertising agencies might want to look into, to help their staffers grow in an informal yet purposeful way. Participants may be encouraged to work out their own program of study, with help from others in the workshop as well as outside resource people.

The Internal Clock of Direct Mail

Many hours are spent trying to get the scheduling of a mailing correct, but how much time is spent on the timing of the message itself?

There is a rhythm to a direct mail package, a pacing and rise and fall that can alter the meaning and intent of the promotion.

For instance, a letter written in very short sentences, or one with single-sentence paragraphs, conveys urgency. This is fine if it's the purpose of the writer to sound hurried or out of breath. But if the package is intended to convey a sense of leisure or thoughtfulness, this accelerated prose style fights the words.

On the other hand, a Latinate prose style, full of elaborate parenthetical remarks and rich descriptions with subordinate clauses as extended as railroad cars on a long freight train, can derail an offer that depends on quick response. It's tempting to reserve your golden prose for the accompanying brochure, but unless you have an art director who likes to set type in seven-point Myopic, you will have to restrain yourself here.

You also have to consider the package as a whole. The most effective packages read as though one person wrote everything. And while the letter may sell stronger than the accompanying brochure, the same rhythms should be evident in both. Rhythm, tempo, and pacing should be carefully watched throughout the creation of a package.

What is *rhythm?* You can define it as that sense of either urgency or casualness discussed above. It's a pulse or pendulum driving home the message; the rate of the pendulum is the *tempo.* The *pacing* is the creative change made in the tempo and rhythm. For instance, your last paragraphs in a letter asking for the order will usually move more quickly, no matter how leisurely the previous paragraphs were. There's no need to create mood here, which is usually done with quieter prose and longer sentences. Now you are building toward a climax and your words call for a faster pacing. (Frequently, the postscript will hark back to an earlier tempo, as if recalling the gist of the message. More often, though, the postscript is a snappy, dramatic closing, designed to clinch the order.)

There's another element of speed and tempo to be watched— *forward movement.* Have you developed your argument briskly, or have you gotten entangled in blind alleys and minutiae? Tight logic, taut story line, and tension will keep the sales story moving ahead.

The internal clock of a package also should be attuned to your audience. An academic readership being confronted with a sales story for a collection of philosophical essays may not be convinced if the direct marketing writer uses incomplete sentences, sentences masquerading as paragraphs, and a galloping, breathless style.

Within the larger overall rhythm of a package, there will fall lesser frequency modulations and interacting cycles. Chronobiologists studying biorhythms refer to "harmonic and relaxation oscillations" in certain periodic patterns. The direct mail writer should be aware of the observed effects of these oscillations. For instance, it appears that tension and relaxation periods are necessary for the well-being of all organisms. Perhaps even the most driving sales letter should loosen up at times, and let the relaxation oscillation take over.

A direct mail package needs variety and the proper balance of low and high points. So instead of an unchanging exhortation, a pause in a long letter may not be unwelcome. This pause may be graphic: an indented paragraph or an underlined subhead or a three-dot leader. It may be a copy device. such as numbered items. It can be the introduction of a long paragraph after a series of short ones.

Every writer has experienced that wonderful instant when a package takes off and assumes a life of its own, becoming an organic whole, with all the elements meshing. It is then that the internal clock of the package starts to tick and then can dictate where and when this break may occur. In some promotions it may not be needed. In others, the sensitive writer will see immediately where the pause that refreshes is called for, without doing harm to the rhythm or tempo of the message.

Listening to the internal rhythms of a direct mail package can give you a promotion that delivers like clockwork.

Self-Help for the Creative: Inspiration at Will

It happens to everybody. Inspiration dries up. The old ingenuity machine runs down. The ideas stop flowing. And even the swipe file won't give up its secrets.

What do you do for ideas when there's a deadline? You can't stop the clock, but you *can* turn on a "creativity generator." There are proven ways to harness those creative abilities within yourself, ways that are consistently productive.

There are as many methods for tapping latent creative potential as there are creative people, but most self-help techniques can be classified in the following categories. They actually do work, but of course they are only as effective as your own motivation, drive, and perseverance. Some seem artificial and contrived until you try them. Others are natural and obvious. You may be employing one of these techniques right now, knowingly or unconsciously. Whichever technique you use, you need not confine yourself to only one; they can all serve as appropriate stimuli.

BRAINSTORMING

When you have no one else around you can turn to for encouragement or inspiration, consider brainstorming. While best known for its use with groups, all the guidelines of brainstorming—with one exception—can be used by people working alone. The exception is *cross-fertilization*, which depends on the ideas of other people. However, for purposes of this individual adaptation, you can practice self-pollination.

Alex F. Osborn, the developer of brainstorming, divided creativity into seven stages:

1. *Orientation*, where the problem is defined and an approach that may aid in solving it is selected
2. *Preparation*, involving gathering facts and all relevant material that may be useful
3. *Analysis*, where you study and analyze the gathered material
4. *Ideation*, when you produce tentative solutions
5. *Incubation*, where conscious effort is suspended while unconscious effort continues
6. *Synthesis*, which involves putting the parts together
7. *Verification*, where the ideas and developed solutions are checked against the problem to determine whether they work

With this as background, when you do individual brainstorming, follow these four basic guidelines:

1. Suspend judgment
2. Freewheel
3. Quantify
4. Combine and improve

You are encouraged to remove any kind of censorship of ideas. Put evaluation aside and try not to edit your ideas. Freewheeling is the process of allowing yourself to drift around the problem. A goal of brainstorming is *quantity*. Try to produce as many ideas as possible. You'll find yourself losing inhibitions and coming up with more original ideas as the flow continues. Combine ideas that occur to you and think of add-ons.

While some of the thoughts and ideas you come up with will be immediately applicable, most will have to be worked out in some way. Some will be discarded, but others may be saved, for use in other projects.

To brainstorm by yourself, sit at your typewriter or computer keyboard and tap out ideas as they come to you, or write them down on a long legal-size pad. It's important to keep the previous ideas in front of you.

This technique works best for problems that have a number of alternative solutions. Areas ripe for solitary brainstorming include locating new markets, designing new applications for present services, dreaming up headlines for new products and services, and pumping new life into declining packages, ads, commercials, products, and markets.

MORPHOLOGICAL ANALYSIS

This technique shapes concepts by taking all the possible independent variables to a problem and trying to combine them in new ways. Some of these ways may already exist, others may be impossible to implement, but some may be innovative and well worth developing.

An example is the promotion of a college loan program. The variables could be:

- *Target audience:* parents, high school seniors, college sophomores
- *Amount of loan:* $5,000, $10,000, $15,000
- *Credit qualifications:* customer in good standing; professional and noncustomer; top-bracket census tract resident and noncustomer
- *Terms:* no collateral, second mortgage, credit card
- *Creative strategy:* computerized letter, self-mailer, 9 × 12 report

The combination of $3 \times 3 \times 3 \times 3 \times 3$ gives you 729 different promotion matrices, many of them readily applicable. For example: Parents plus $10,000 plus customer in good standing plus second mortgage plus computerized letter yields a warm personalized letter from a local branch offer.

One way to handle morphological analysis is to note all the variables on 3×5 cards, which then can be shuffled about and sorted into different combinations of variables. A computer software company called Soft Path Systems [phone: (503) 342–3439] has developed Brainstormer, a program for CP/M and IBM compatibles based on morphological analysis, which allows the user to benefit from this technique without having to fill out any cards.

ATTRIBUTE LISTING

First identify all the characteristics or attributes of a problem—a mailing, an ad campaign, or an offer—then examine each separately with an eye toward possible modification.

You can apply attribute listing to a project such as the improvement of an insurance mailing. First list all the attributes:

Window envelope (6×9)
Corner card only
Indicia
Name and address showthrough
Personalized order form
Personalized two-page letter
Four-page brochure
Lift letter

Then examine every attribute to see whether any changes may be made. This can develop into fundamental improvements. For example:

1. Use a No. 10 envelope.
2. Put a teaser on the front.
3. Use metered postage.
4. Show a deadline or a cash figure through a window.
5. Turn the order form into a certificate.
6. Shorten the letter.
7. Combine the brochure with the letter.
8. Turn the lift letter into a note on a business card.

Now go one step further. Instead of concerning yourself with minor attributes, think big. Apply the dominant attributes of one situation to another area.

For example, the idea of office cooperatives or condominiums developed from an apartment concept that spread to businesses who had traditionally rented their office space. The idea of checking accounts for mutual funds and brokerage customers grew out of a redefinition of what these services really were and a good look at competitive banking services.

MODIFICATION

To stimulate new ideas and to question current ideas and objectives, Alex F. Osborn developed nine basic categories for modification. His original generalized checklist had these main headings: put to other uses, adapt, modify, magnify, "minify" (reduce or lessen in scale), substitute, rearrange, reverse, and combine. A modification of this modification technique is *lateral thinking and PO* (PO is a way of thinking), developed and popularized by Edward de Bono.

Dr. de Bono's method is a freewheeling mode of thought designed to encourage the chance interaction of ideas. Traditional analytical thinking usually has two possible outcomes—acceptance or rejection of an idea. So new ideas and innovations are often rejected. On the other hand, lateral thinking defers this yes-no evaluation and may show a way out of a no-go situation. For example, ask yourself if your envelope legend might not work better as a brochure headline. Could your sales letter fit on the outside of an envelope? Don't say no; say maybe, and pursue the idea.

FORCED RELATIONSHIPS

Several techniques use the concept of forced relationships to stimulate ideas. By forcing a relationship between normally unrelated services or concepts, you can make sparks.

One of these methods is called the *catalog technique*, which sounds like something direct marketers should be familiar with! It takes words, objects, or pictures from catalogs or magazines and randomly combines them with other objects, words, or pictures.

Both elements are then considered together and a new relationship is forced between the two to give a totally new concept.

For instance, taking the word *lamp* from one headline and combining it with the word *desk* from another headline gives you obvious combinations like "desk lamp" or "illuminated desk." But wait a minute. What about a desk with a drawer that lights up when opened? What about a lamp on a clipboard? What about a teller's window that lights up when the teller is available? Obviously, this is a useful technique when you are looking for new ideas.

Another forced relationship technique is *listing*. Think of a general subject area and list objects or ideas associated with it. Number these ideas and then consider the first item in relationship to all the others. Do the same with the second item, and so on.

If you had to develop new promotions to the customers of a bank, you might list and number the current products being sold: (1) savings accounts; (2) checking accounts; (3) credit cards; (4) ATM; (5) personal loans; (6) safe deposit boxes. Then start by considering the relationship between savings accounts and checking accounts.

Could you combine the two? Introduce a savings account with checks? Automatic deductions from credit-card balances into savings accounts? Free safe deposit boxes for checking accounts with a minimum balance?

Another forced relationship technique is the *forced object method*, which is a way to focus your attention on the problem. First select the fixed element and then focus your attention on some other element around you. This is designed to set up a chain of free association.

For instance, if you have to expand marketing uses for a house list, think of the list as the fixed element and the random element as the first thing you see in front of you—your typewriter, perhaps. The ideas flowing from this forced relationship may include ideas about selling typewriters to the house list, renting the list to an office supplies company, or offering a free typing course in connection with some promotion.

Free up your mind to wander away from the original forced relationship, which, of course, was just a launching pad to get you thinking. Play games with the word "typing," for instance. That leads you to *typecasting*—rent the list to a subscription theater.

PakSA

Another idea-starting technique is PakSA. Developed by J. W. Taylor for the Packing Corporation of America, PakSA (PackCorp Scientific Approach) is a nine-step list technique:

1. Pick a problem. Define and state it.
2. Collect knowledge. Research and study.
3. Organize knowledge. Sort your information.
4. Refine knowledge. Look for patterns, cause and effect.
5. Digest the knowledge. Put it aside and ruminate on it.
6. Produce ideas. Study the problem until ideas begin to emerge.
7. Rework ideas. Evaluate the ideas. Challenge them.
8. Put ideas to work. Communicate your ideas to superiors or clients.
9. Repeat the process.

ROLE PLAYING

Another technique is playing the role of your customer or prospect (a "subself"), in order to identify with him. Some scientific evidence shows that certain people perform significantly better when this creative "subself" is in operation.

The technique called synectics uses this method in a procedure known as personal analogy. Here a person imagines himself to be the object or materials with which he is working. This way, he learns and understands more about the characteristics of these materials and so more about the various uses to which they can be adapted.

Copywriters employ role playing when they ask themselves, "What would a young parent of two children find appealing about this insurance policy?" By taking on another role, you give yourself license to think differently and set aside censorship and any self-editing rigidities that can inhibit ideas.

Through these simple procedures, you can enhance your own creativity and stimulate the creativity of others to simplify and enrich your work.

New Approaches to Brainstorming

If a direct marketing manager were to say to her staff, "I want you to go wild and say anything that comes into your head," she may confidently expect to get nothing but a cynical smile for her pains. Yet every week, otherwise conservative and undemonstrative direct marketing professionals are going wild in meetings, at the express invitation of their bosses.

It's all part of the growing use of systemized group procedures to solve problems and stimulate creativity. And since many of these group procedures emphasize loosening up thought processes and not evaluating ideas during a meeting, the result is a freewheeling, anything-goes atmosphere.

Of course, business meetings have always been with us. But today's sophisticated group procedures for stimulating creativity go beyond the classic business conference with its tension, rancor, and rigidity. These new procedures for the more effective production of usable ideas, when used correctly, can enhance communication, break down barriers of competitiveness or secretiveness, and discipline the mind of each participant.

Brainstorming

Brainstorming is an ideal way to lower barriers to problem solving. The bank had a problem: How to announce the closing of an unprofitable branch while still holding on to its customers. The direct marketing department was given the assignment, and a brainstorming session was held.

STEP 1: PROBLEM STATEMENT

First the problem was stated: "Close a branch without losing customers." Then the problem was restated as a "how-to" sentence: "How to close the branch without losing customers."

STEP 2: RESTATEMENTS

The basic problem was then restated, identifying as many different facets of the problem as possible. Each restatement was phrased in terms of how to do something.

1. How to announce the closing of the branch
2. How to announce the closing to customers
3. How to avoid losing customers
4. How to . . . [and so on, as many as possible]

STEP 3: BRAINSTORMINGS

Restatements were chosen and "brainstormed." How can we announce the closing of the branch to customers and keep them happy? Suggestions came fast and furious.

1. Direct mail
2. Radio
3. Gift for switching account to another branch of their choice
4. Special hours at nearest branch for switching customers
5. Thirty days' free safe deposit box rental
6. Thirty days' free checking account
7. Special newsletter to all branch employees with ideas on how to welcome old customers
8. Telemarketing campaign offering alternative branches

STEP 4: WILDEST IDEA

The group took the wildest idea from the brainstorming session to further loosen up their thinking. It also produced some giggles and refreshened the group.

332. Keep the other branches in the area open around the clock.
333. Keep all branches open seven days a week.
334. Open all branches on holidays.
335. Offer a holiday special to "evicted" customers: "Christmas in July" or "Banksgiving/Thanksgiving."

336. Hold an old-fashioned block party for people moving to other branches.

While many ideas were not usable, several good ones were generated as the result of this brainstorming session.

Brainstorming has the advantage of encouraging individuals in a group to piggyback on one another's ideas and suggestions. It allows participants to communicate easily without getting trapped by any bureaucratic set of regulations. It fosters individual creativity while opening up new channels of communication within the group.

Although it has since moved into other areas, brainstorming was specifically developed to aid advertising people. It was originated in 1938 by Alex F. Osborn to achieve "organized ideation" in his agency, Batten, Barton, Durstine & Osborn, the same agency where direct marketing pioneer John Caples (author of the great mail order ad: "They laughed when I sat down at the piano") worked for so many years.

Osborn considered the creative problem-solving process in three parts: (1) fact finding, (2) idea finding, and (3) solution finding. The second part—idea finding—is where brainstorming comes in. Stated succinctly, it is a method for coming up with ideas without regard to their evaluation.

For the most effective generation of ideas, Osborn proposed two major principles: judgment must be deferred, and quantity breeds quality. He also set forth four essential rules for a brainstorming session:

1. *Criticism is not allowed.* Defer judgment and put off all criticism and evaluation.
2. *Free wheeling is welcomed.* People can relax and use their imagination, because they are relieved of any responsibility for evaluation.
3. *Quantity is wanted.* The more ideas suggested, the greater the probability that an original one will come up.
4. *Combination and improvement are sought.* This motivates participants to build on other ideas. It offsets any embarrassment someone may feel at not coming up with the idea first.

Brainstorming can generate some very wild ideas, but it offers solid advantages. It enlists and develops a spirit of enthusiasm. It multiplies individual effort in solving problems. It supplements the formal, judicial conference, which can often be barren of fresh thinking. And it induces a more creative attitude in the individual, developing a readiness to think freely.

Brainstorming Variations

SYNECTICS

An interesting version of brainstorming is synectics, which originated with William J. J. Gordon in 1944. It uses metaphors and analogies in a systematic way to achieve creative results. Together with former marketing specialist George M. Prince, Gordon formed Synectics, Inc., to provide training in this technique, which is used in companies and schools today.

Synectics attempts to engage nonrational processes through the purposeful use of metaphors and analogies. It also encourages rational and logical processes.

Students of the creative process have long been aware of the importance and influence of metaphorical imagery in creativity. A famous example is the nineteenth-century German chemist, Friedrich August Kekule von Stradonitz, who came up with the benzene ring theory, an essential part of modern organic chemistry, by thinking of a snake swallowing its tail. Alexander Graham Bell used the direct analogy of the ear as a machine, which became the telephone receiver. And the Wright brothers based their experiments on turning and stabilizing the airplane on observations of buzzards keeping their balance in flight.

The synectics process has three major segments. The first defines, elaborates, analyzes, and understands the problem. The second applies four operational mechanisms to the process:

1. *Personal analogy,* in which the individual identifies with the object with which he is working
2. *Direct analogy,* where parallel knowledge, facts, or technology from one field are used in another (medical diagnostic

procedures may serve as an analogy to solve problems of credit checking)

3. *Symbolic analogy*, which uses a visual image to describe the problem (referring to orchestra and balcony seats, for instance, when developing the tiers of a new insurance plan)
4. *Fantasy analogy*, which goes beyond known physical laws to explore possibilities (could a store expand by pushing out its walls like a balloon?)

The third segment of the problem-solving process tries to "force a fit" between what the group has arrived at and the problem on which it is working.

A synectics group includes a leader, a "client-expert," and four or five participants. The leader, trained in the synectics process, runs the session and records all the ideas on large sheets of paper. He himself does not contribute ideas. The client-expert takes over the problem. The meeting is designed to produce solutions that are acceptable to her, and she has the right to veto any avenue of exploration.

Synectics requires careful training in an elaborate sequence of steps if it is to be effective.

OTHER GROUP PROCESSES

Another procedure is *creative problem solving*. Based on several of Alex F. Osborn's ideas, it emphasizes deferred judgment and brainstorming and assigns a basic role of checklists. This procedure also has an elaborate training program in fact finding, problem finding, idea finding, solution finding, and acceptance finding.

Still another method, the interdisciplinary analog laboratory, is designed to stimulate creativity and develop thinking along alternative paths by bringing together participants from different disciplines or areas of expertise. They discuss possible solutions to a problem in terms of analogy from their own background, with a group leader feeding back this discussion to all participants.

Many organizations are exploring techniques for stimulating creativity on a group level. General Electric's Creative Engineering Program uses brainstorming and other problem-solving techniques.

Its graduates have produced patents at about three times the rate of nonparticipant engineers.

Coca-Cola's program uses brainstorming, synectics, attribute analysis, systems analysis, morphological analysis, and the generation of alternatives. Hotpoint's variety of techniques includes a method that helps participants develop a sensitivity to the problems.

All these techniques, individual and group alike, appear to share certain common conditions. One of these is free thinking. This encourages the mind to wander in any direction without any inhibitions. In this free state, you can often perceive similarities between concepts, systems, and techniques. You can catch these occurrences most easily when you are in a state of readiness, which comes with practice. The open mind or willingness to look at every possibility before rejecting anything is also helpful in enhancing the creative process. The last two conditions are alertness and discipline, allowing you to put into action what you have just learned.

So the next time you have the job of coming up with a package that will beat the control or an ad that will pull in inquiries at an unheard-of rate, have your creative strategy ready for use.

By being aware of and harnessing your personal creative resources, you can make them work for you at your convenience and come up with new ideas whenever you have to, without writer's block or other impediments to inspiration.

Use a Theme to Organize and Support Your Ideas

A theme, a motif, can be useful in many direct marketing programs. Basically, a theme is "the one big idea"—the direct marketer's message. A theme deals with universal concepts: freedom, power, courage, ambition, love, money. ("All men are brothers" for a fund-raising appeal; "Travel broadens the mind" for a European tour.) While not all packages or ads call for a theme, you'll find it can be helpful when you must:

• *Generate ideas.* Leafing through a collection of proverbs, quotations, or maxims can actually spark that flash of insight you need to bring together a promotion. For instance, "Habits are at first cobwebs, at last cables," can set the stage for a subscription effort for a new magazine that is attempting to compete with a popular old standard.

• *Build a slogan* to epitomize your proposition. When you're looking for a tag line to an ad, a dramatic statement in a superscription, or the closing words to a commercial, you can articulate an often elusive concept with a simple, even clichéd statement. Try not to be pretentious though, remembering the Hollywood wisecrack: "If you want to send a message, use Western Union."

As a collection followup to phoned-in donation promises after a national telethon, this gentle reminder as an envelope teaser can help bring those checks in: "A gift much expected is paid, not given."

• *Stay on track and sustain momentum.* A theme need not be stated in so many words to work. For example, a mailing package is a very complex production that can have you going in a dozen directions at once. Use an adage to help herd your ideas and come to the point quickly when you have trouble focusing on the goal. (What's the precise result you're after? What is the mailing's objective? What is its main—not sole—appeal?) Write the maxim down, keep it in front of you, and use it as a benchmark while editing, to make sure you're not straying. It can also help you unify and so get the most impact from copy points, headlines, postscripts, sidebars, and lead-ins, as well as help you avoid splitting a message between letter and brochure.

Try weaving the idea that "the early bird catches the worm" into your charter introductory subscription offer, and follow through in copy, captions, and graphics. For a home study course, a theme of "It's never too late to learn" appears trite and obvious. But as a tacit motif powering your package, it should help you set the stage for your pitch, give you an idea for the format of the package, help you select lists, and allow you to strike the right emotional appeal.

Direct Marketing Lessons From the Performing Arts

Performing arts companies, civic theater groups, and symphony orchestras depend heavily on subscription promotions through direct mail. In these austere days, even a richly endowed organization must turn to subscribers and audiences for a substantial portion of operating revenue. So to make sure the muses are heard, and to bring about more performances and longer seasons, the promoter of opera, concerts, and plays has become a shrewd marketer, using many of the techniques that profit-making organizations rely on—including direct marketing—to sell seasonal memberships on a cost-effective basis.

In adapting direct marketing techniques to the special needs of concert events, performing arts groups, and resident stage companies, promoters have evolved their own variations on a theme. It might be wise for the profit-oriented direct marketer to examine these often ingenious and productive methods and see how they may be used in the service of lesser-known muses, like Indicia, the patroness of direct mail, and Responsa, the guiding spirit of bountiful replies.

1. *Ask for renewals early.* The Alley Theater of Houston, Texas, starts asking for subscription renewals at least two plays before the current season's ending. (Thousands of its subscribers renew annually.)

A performing arts organization usually requires at least 50 percent renewal. Anything less, and the company itself may not survive. So some symphony orchestras present flowers to subscribers who have renewed early. In one year, the Minnesota Orchestra began asking for renewals on January 11, several months ahead of time. By March it had harvested $451,000 in cash, to earn interest until the new season began that fall. Its letter to subscribers that year began: "First chance to renew your seats for the Gala 75th Anniversary Season." No special break was offered, other than "You can relax knowing your seats are secure even before other subscribers are given this announcement."

2. *Use the phones.* Shortly before the beginning of a new season, the Cleveland Orchestra assigned one telephone solicitor to new business. In one month he produced $19,407 worth of series ticket sales. A good subscription renewal in the theater includes a heavy phone campaign, to either the slower renewer's home or office. (An advantage the nonprofit marketer often has over the for-profit organization is the depth of information available on subscribers, who include third- and even fourth-generation members.)

One well-known symphony orchestra tells its telephoners to ask for criticism and find out why people have dropped out. This basic research often leads to a sale as the recalcitrant subscriber gets it out of her system and renews, simply out of gratitude for having been listened to.

3. *Offer a grace period.* Borrowed from the insurance companies, this technique may find its way back to the mail order insurance companies! A repertory group will contact lapsed subscribers, giving them an extension of time to renew, with the understanding that perhaps there was a reason for being late—extended vacation or urgent personal business. The solicitation hints that nobody who knows anything about the forthcoming season would be so gauche as to not renew. Another method is the last-minute offer of the best available seats on a priority basis before the general public gets its orders filled.

No former subscriber is ever considered a lost cause, at least not until the curtain rises on the new season. Some performing arts have mined older lists of lapsed subscribers with reported success rates of up to 20 percent.

4. *Consider direct mail a primary medium.* Even allowing for the budgetary magic of a nonprofit, third-class mailing permit, direct mail plays an essential role in a marketing plan. It is a powerful force in selling subscriptions to a season at the opera or symphony.

In one season, the New York Philharmonic sold only 2,230 new series ticket subscriptions through newspaper ads. Switching to a heavy mail campaign, it unearthed more than 10,000 subscribers.

In one four-year period, the Pittsburgh Symphony Orchestra

went from a $35,000 annual budget, which pulled in $200,000 worth of sales and renewals, to a $75,000 budget, which grossed $918,000.

5. *Offer a hefty discount.* By offering one out of every five plays free to season subscribers, one repertory theater achieved a 125 percent season ticket gain. An additional $500,000 over the previous year in ticket sales was earned. And since discounts are not graven in stone, you can change your policy according to the situation. San Francisco's American Conservatory Theater offered a 50 percent discount in its early years, cutting the discount down gradually until it disappeared entirely. Thanks to the new audience the early generous discount had created, the theater still enjoyed standing-room-only sales.

Often forced to operate lean and mean, performing arts groups are successfully using direct marketing techniques to sell season subscriptions. By getting back to the basics, they're getting back into the black, and they're teaching other direct marketers that it is still essential to sell hard, make a good offer, and ask for the order.

Secrets of Fund Raising

Fund raisers, faced with tiny budgets and a well that may have been gone to once too many times, surely rank among the most successful practitioners of direct response promotion. Perhaps adversity sparks a higher degree of ingenuity, but even multimillion-dollar advertising agencies with their large crews of gifted strategists and conceptualizers would be hard put to match some of the fund raisers' ideas. These are some of my favorites. They can pay off for you too, no matter what you are promoting.

THE BROWN BAG

How to touch the hearts and pockets of alumni weary of the same old college cry for money? A Midwestern alumni association sent out a brown paper bag imprinted with a message: "Next week carry your lunch instead of buying it. Then give the [money] you save each day to the Alumni Fund." No letter—the outside of the bag served as both the letter and the outer envelope. Inside the envelope: a business reply envelope.

Within the limitations of postal regulations, you may want to explore imprinting other unusual mailing devices: book jackets or menus as self-mailers, Jiffy Bags with long advertising messages, pay envelopes, shopping bags, even cereal boxes!

THE PARTY THAT NEVER WAS

A small Southern college decided *not* to hold a dinner dance for its alumni, and bragged about it in a fund-raising package—which included tickets and a program. The letter itemized some of the expenses that the recipient saved—babysitter, dinner-jacket rental, gasoline—and suggested that a check for some of the money saved would make a wonderful donation.

You may want to promote cable TV within a community by throwing a theater party and carefully listing the expenses of a night on the town, with the obvious comparison of a cozy night watching HBO or the Movie Channel. ("The family that stays home together saves together.")

THE LIST UPON WHICH I HAVE FOUND YOUR NAME

A sectarian college sends alumni a proof copy of its donor honor roll and asks them to check the spelling of names. An Eastern college created an alumni yearbook, with photos and listings for each alumnus; graduates were asked to update their achievements. In both instances, a pitch was made for funds, of course.

A subscription renewal effort based on a copy of the subscriber's mailing label may ask the prospect to check for correct address and spelling. An "office record" of accounts in good standing might ask the slow-paying customer to check for his name and to send in a check to ensure being included (with the tacit reminder that his credit standing might be in jeopardy.)

THE LEVEL OF GIVING DESERVES A GIFT

Membership programs offer donors tangible recognition for their generous gifts, scaled to reflect the donation. A black-tie dinner might honor fat-cat donors, while a less elaborate luncheon might award the more modest giver.

Instead of giving all subscribers a pocket calculator or a telephone, scale the gifts according to the length of the subscription or the time it takes to respond to your offer. Subscribers who come in earlier get a nicer gift than those who drift in a month or so later.

Frequently, direct marketing campaigns are conceived without an eye on the budget, and everyone is surprised when the invoices mount up. Instead, take a tip from the ingenious, harried fund raiser, and see what you can do while making do.

CHAPTER 7

Direct Mail Diagnosis: On the Road to Better Performance

How to Hold a Postmortem on a Promotion

It's easy to tell when you've got a turkey on your hands. When a promotion bombs heavily, it sets off seismographs halfway around the world, babies whimper at the sight of your commercial, and the post office quarantines your organization.

At times like these, there may be a hurried review of the promotion to find out why it died, but it probably would be more in the nature of an inquisition or a court-martial than a calm, scientific examination of the facts.

Rarely, however, will there be an attempt to run down the reasons for the lukewarm performance of a mailing or ad that should have done well and just didn't quite come up to expectations.

And yet the semisoft promotion is the only one that really demands probes, scalpels, and analytical tests. A careful autopsy on a mediocre mailing or a disappointing ad can often be more revealing than a hasty proceeding after an obvious failure.

Some of the questions to ask might include:

• *Was the market too competitive* to sustain still another foray? Did you get there too late with too little? (Another sweepstakes to a list assaulted with sweeps or a catalog to a market buffeted by every other catalog.)

• *Was the offer too complicated?* Too legalistic? Promotions for financial services and products must be okayed by several layers of lawyers, each of whom may feel impelled to add something to the pot. Was the final stew indigestible to the consumer?

• *Is the ad or mailing being judged fairly?* Errors in testing procedures may lead to wrong conclusions. Perhaps you may not have allowed for the vagaries of sociodemographic factors or the time of the year.

• *Was there too much natural resistance to be overcome?* You may not have made your offer as attractive as possible. It may just sit there, in the hope that prospects will respond.

• *Did you select the right offer?* Surprisingly, free gifts sometimes can lower response. For instance, offering a variety of similar gifts makes it difficult to make a choice, and the prospect puts aside your offer, intending to make a selection some other time—which never comes.

• *Did your payment method depress response?* Cash with order, for instance, is much less appealing than a billing arrangement or installment terms or credit card.

• *Did you make it easy to order?* Is your coupon really user friendly? Does it say, "Clip me" or "Skip me"?

• *Have you listened to your customers?* Was your mailing to your customer list in line with past experience? If your customers are used to a free trial offer, did you offer it this time out? And did you listen to *potential* customers? Did you study the publications going to prospects? Did you read the ads and the features and write your ad using the same vocabulary?

• *Did you perceive a product need that really didn't exist?* Is your product or service reaching the end of its life cycle? Are you pushing water beds instead of home computers?

• *Did you use the wrong size ad?* A one-column or two-column doesn't work all that much better than a four-inch or a three-inch ad when you're selling a single product at a low price.

• *Was your ad sitting in the wrong place?* Ads closer to the front of the magazine often work better than those in the back. (There are exceptions.) And right-hand pages pull much better than left-hand pages.

• *Does your promotion have integrity?* Is it organically whole? Or does it look and sound like it was put together by a carpool? Did you use a creative strategy, or was the promotion based on instinct and "experience"? A creative-strategy document will focus thinking and isolate the one big idea that will meet your marketing objectives.

• *Did the copywriter really do his homework?* Good direct marketing copy is advocacy journalism. It digs out the facts and translates them into customer benefits in vivid language that is understandable.

• *Did you allow for human inertia?* Offering a little inducement for quick response, such as a small gift or cents-off deal, will often do wonders for a sluggish promotion.

A careful postmortem can help resurrect a listless promotion, and the lessons learned may well give your next mailing or ad that extra push needed to put it over the top. So don't give up on those mediocre mailings and so-so ads. Analyze them, see where you may have gone wrong, and profit from an otherwise unprofitable promotion.

What to Do When the Flow Chart Dries Up

How do you keep track of orders while filling them? How do you make use of the information received (name and address of customer, source or order, amount, date), while reducing it to reports and graphs and discernible patterns?

The sort of scorekeeping we do in direct marketing calls for a careful system if we don't want to get buried in paper. The oldest and most popular approach to analyzing the flow of orders is the flow chart. In this method, you start with the different kinds of orders coming in, and you follow the flow of data step by step until it leaves in the form of completed orders, invoices, and reports, such as printouts.

Sometimes decision points are shown. These are places in the process where someone has to do something. The first one, for example, may be the point at which somebody sorts the orders according to source. What users have found is that there are also problem points—disadvantages—to this system. The flow chart can actually hypnotize the user into believing that everything is flowing smoothly, as though by charting an activity we make that activity perfect—something like accepting an airline schedule as a real-world timetable. Flow-chart users face five major problems.

1. *Mechanics over matter.* The flow chart has a way of concentrating attention on the mechanics of the operation; the form and quality of both input and output are ignored. So rather than taking a second look at the order form, to see if it needs improvement, you automatically assume that it's fine and that the information is coming in loud and clear. The same assumption can be made about the way the information is going out: invoices, acknowledgments, and requisitions are as well developed as they'll ever be. The focus is on the order from the time it's received until the time it's

completed, as though it came into the world completely formed and matured.

2. *Squeezing in instead of sprucing up.* Another case of not challenging the system. You plan the flow of work in and around the existing plumbing, instead of asking whether this or that pipe is necessary. By going with the flow of established methods instead of questioning the existing arrangements, you may be in danger of not taking advantage of more efficient methods. So a long-used way of entering an order that may be a carryover of precomputer days becomes further entrenched.

3. *Slicing and dicing rather than melding and welding.* Here's that old self-hypnosis problem again. The flow chart takes on a personality of its own and you begin to look at the whole flow of operations as a chartable series of disconnected, discrete, and separate steps connected in a fixed sequence. *Example:* The flow chart decrees that the first step in order handling is to note the source of the order; the second step, to read the rest of it; and the third, to pass it on to the next department. But isn't there a relationship among these three steps? So while the source is being duly noted, couldn't something else be happening to the order at the same time, like checking the amount of the remittance or transcribing any credit-card information?

4. *Clicking instead of clocking.* Not enough emphasis is placed on timing. Flow charts tend to look at stops (places where work comes to a halt), rather than stopwatches. Timing ought to be part of the work-flow analysis.

5. *Cramping instead of creating.* There's nothing especially interesting about creating a flow chart. In fact, it's downright dull. So after designing two or three of them, the direct marketing manager is inclined to look for a cookie cutter. Rather than look at the problem as something to be approached creatively, he goes to his files and photocopies a previous solution.

There are other, perhaps better techniques for order-flow analysis than flow charts. Critical path methods and mathematical modeling systems are being used in the mail order business. Sometimes, though, the operation is too small to justify these elaborate methods. So the analyst returns to the flow chart. But this time, perhaps he ought to go about it differently. Before designing the flow chart, he ought to ask questions. Are all the reports being generated absolutely meaningful? And is the flow of information being treated as a group of isolated and insignificant routines, instead of an organic happening that can deliver decision-making data more efficiently?

A Quick Survey of Direct Marketing Mistakes

Aside from head-slapping goofs like reverse printing an order form so that only white ink could be used to fill it out, or printing an envelope on paper so slick that a label could never adhere, direct marketing is remarkably tolerant of errors.

However, even the most diligent of marketers can make certain mistakes that will prove perilous to the bottom line. Here is a Museum of Horrors with some of the most horrible. But remember, as Cicero said, "Any man may make a mistake, but only a fool will continue in it."

• *Hoping a list is up-to-date.* Americans move around a lot, and to think that a mailing list is as permanent as the Washington Monument is like relying on a rope of sand. A list has to be constantly corrected in order to be useful. So when you're offered a cut-rate list, ask about up-to-dateness as well as recency, frequency, and size of purchase.

• *Working out the offer after the fact.* Sometimes a brilliant idea or a clever headline or a striking format comes first. Hold off. Don't write a word or design an envelope until you've painstakingly constructed an offer. In fact, do as the oldtimers did: Design your order form first. It's an effective discipline that forces you to look at your proposition, your pricing, your product. And a simple way to articulate your offer is to write a Johnson box—the superscription over the salutation in a sales letter. It's an exercise that many copywriters use to encapsulate in a dozen words or so what they're selling.

• *Not asking for the order.* It has happened. You fall in love with your words. The art director has a beautiful design. The product is magical. And the orders never come in. Oooh—you forgot to ask the prospect to take action. Never confuse the shadow for the substance. Be crass: Ask for the order.

• *Ignoring the inquirer.* Over-the-transom or white mail is a problem for direct marketers. How to credit it? There's no key. No code. Where did it come from? Why is the person interfering with my marketing plan? Treating the inquirer like a long-lost child rather than an unwanted orphan can do wonders for your bottom line. And if a lot of unaccountable mail comes in, check your promotions. Perhaps a key was left out, and you're not giving credit where credit is due, which might make all the difference in the world at rollout time.

• *Not making the layout and copy complement each other.* A subtle layout uneasily houses hard-sell language. A buckeye layout wars with soft, leisurely copy. How often have you come across Jekyll-and-Hyde marketing, where the copywriter and art director each mailed in their assignments from opposite ends of the earth? Perhaps it's time to use copy-art teams, rather than autonomous creative people who refuse to work together.

• *Testing the untestable.* A national magazine was famous for testing things like the color of the stamps on its direct mail package and the use of commas versus colons after salutations. Split tests were constructed and charts were carefully kept . . . and the results were never quite clear.

Keep your objectives firmly in mind and don't be distracted by the imponderable, imprecise, or impenetrable. Return to the basics and refuse to be seduced by statistics for statistics' sake. Remember the variation of Heisenberg's Theory of Indeterminancy: "The observed phenomenon is altered by the observation."

• *Watching your pennies.* Trying to save money without considering your goals and objectives is short-sighted. Yet many managers who wish to impress the boss will try to budget way below sensible levels. The result: "junk mail" poorly designed, sloppily written, carelessly printed, hastily mailed, and indifferently received.

Questions and Answers

Q: We want to test several prices. How many price levels should we try for?
A: At least two. If you have an established product that you're marketing to a new audience, or a new product to your old customers, you want to know what price would have the best impact. If you have an established product you're selling to your old market at a nice price, try for three price levels: "good, better, best." It's surprising how many old customers will accept a much higher price, if the blow is softened by good reasonable copy.

When offering a new product to a new audience, use at least three different price levels here too. You might be pleasantly surprised at the highest-price acceptance rate. *Important:* The price levels should be significantly different, otherwise you won't learn a thing!

Q: How much profit can we expect to see with a first-time-ever offer?
A: Direct marketing savant Maxwell Sackheim always preached the power of the second act. That is, your curtain opener, or initial offer, should not be the sole reason for your being in the business. You're either in direct marketing for the long haul, building a reputation and a client list, or you're a "street hustler," peddling merchandise from a truck.

If you're serious about direct marketing, think of your first ad or mailing as *buying* names, not *selling* merchandise or services. It's only with your second, third, fourth, and fifth promotion that you'll begin to see daylight. And in publishing, it's your magazine or newsletter renewal business that will really pay the way. In fact, the short-term offer is perhaps the ideal way to measure the long-term profit potential of a customer list very quickly.

So, armed with this long-range outlook, prepare to invest in new customers and not see any real profit immediately. If you have no experience, keep careful figures and watch the percentage of repeat business. That way you'll learn how much a new name is worth to you. And be prepared to experience a certain degree of attrition.

In time, you'll find that a small group of repeat buyers (probably no more than 20 percent of your entire list) will be responsible for 80 percent of your sales.

Q: We're seeing more letters without salutations. Is this a trend?

A: If it is, it's been a trend for seventy years or so. Many years ago, a writer caught between "Dear Friend" and "Dear Reader" chose to use no salutation at all. He used a standard headline instead. Finding that a bit graceless, another writer thought of "Good Morning" as *his* salutation. And still another creative soul in the glorious era of $0.022 third-class mail, started her letters without further ado: "If you're wondering . . . how we can offer you this wonderful electric icebox for only . . ." The first three words—"If you're wondering . . ."—sat in the space formerly reserved for "Dear Friend."

With computerized salutations now the norm, some alternative direct marketers have decided this form of personalization has taken the letter out of the realm of personal communication entirely. In recognition of this new era of impersonality, these contrarians are sending letters that begin abruptly, sans salutation, sans headlines.

Some observers believe there's an unfinished look to these unsalutated letters. That gentle knock on the door or throat-clearing bid for attention is no longer there, and the tradition of the courteous greeting has been scrapped for a gruff, unexpected, falsely "all business" sales talk.

Now the pendulum is due to swing back for another go-around of old-fashioned salutations—until another direct marketer, searching for a different way to start a letter, will rediscover the power of precipitous persuasion.

Q: What is a "third-party" guarantee?

A: It's a reinforcement of your own guarantee by an outside

organization. For instance, a sweepstakes mailing might include as part of its package a letter from a bank officer affirming that the prize money is on deposit or is being held in escrow in the bank. Or a seal of approval by a testing laboratory might attest to a product's dependability. This form of endorsement might also be a letter from an educational institution approving a textbook, or a government agency signing off on a financial product offer (the IRS, for instance, has a form letter to be included in IRA presentations).

The Four Phases of Mail Counting

Even hardened veterans of direct marketing admit they still get goose bumps when waiting for the first results of a new campaign to arrive. Observers have broken down the mail-count routine into four phases: anxiety, excitement, depression, acceptance.

ANXIETY

Anxiety marks that period between the mail drop or ad breaking and the first responses. At one time, when the post office could be depended on to deliver mail promptly, it was possible to know within a day or two when orders would begin to be received. But mail delivery today is a much more casual event and the direct marketer is often surprised when the first responses do arrive. This anxiety is sometimes called the Noah Syndrome, because you're waiting for the dove to return with the olive leaf.

EXCITEMENT

With each day bringing more responses, you enter the second phase of the mail count: excitement. While you may have counted each piece of mail individually at first, the sacks of mail keep piling up, and you now have to weigh mail by batches or count letter trays. You can't afford to be sloppy at this time, because a rollout may depend on an accurate count of returns. It's strange how the care and precision that went into the selection and breakout of lists can often disappear when responses come flooding in. There can be a trap here for the unwary who make predictions on the strength of two or three days' receipts, instead of carefully charting the flow over a period of time.

In this interval, an important anniversary is marked: the Doubling Date. Depending on what type of promotion it is, you can anticipate 50 percent of the expected returns to have been received by a certain day. Years ago, experts were quick to say that the doubling date was ten days from the mail drop, or perhaps fourteen days, or maybe fifteen. This gentle uncertainty became almost hysterical irresolution as the once-dependable postal system took on a life of its own, with rhythms and frequencies that changed haphazardly. Today, direct marketers use their own experience, knowledge of postal service vagaries, and insight into the particular promotion to set a doubling date, which may not be universally accepted.

DEPRESSION

Because of the nature of mail, there always seems to be a time early on when it looks like you've got a winner on your hands. But this can just be the breakup of ice floes, where something was clogging distribution. In a brief while (sometimes *very* brief), the mail trickles down to a few pieces, and depression sets in. You've got a loser. Elation turns to gloom. You begin to dread the inevitable report to your superiors, your accountant, your bank, your shareholders. You doubt your writing abilities, your marketing skills, your sense of the marketplace. Is it too late to change occupations? Perhaps very early retirement is in the offing.

ACCEPTANCE

Then somebody gives you a preliminary report, decorated with a chart. Your promotional instincts are alerted. A pattern has become evident. And while you don't have a smash hit, you do have a new control. And so, the last phase—acceptance—is entered. You're now calm enough to look at the results objectively, and you begin to make plans for the next campaign. Because there is a chance, a possibility, that you might be able to pull off a real triumph—if you just noodle around a little more with the offer, change the headline, and redo the graphics.

When a Control Is Chewed to Bits

Some controls that have enjoyed long lives seem to lose vitality at the end of a much-honored existence. They just don't seem to have the pep that they enjoyed in their lusty youth, and they're dethroned by the first new test that swaggers into town. Is it fair to retire these old-timers on the basis of a single test, or should they be granted a second chance to prove themselves?

One reason that's given for the demise of these once-mighty packages is a changing marketplace. That may be true in some instances, especially if you're selling something that's technologically oriented, such as a home-study electronics course. But there may be another reason: What often happens is that a successful mailing package, originally designed as a complete entity, with every part contributing something—from the order form that repeats the offer to the letter that directs the reader to the order form—has been chewed to bits.

Over the years, many hands may have changed the control package. A new marketing manager may have suggested a new and improved offer. A production manager may have changed the grade of paper. An art director may have updated a typeface. And a copywriter may have improved the envelope legend and the opening paragraph of the letter. Others may have altered the brochure, or added a lift letter.

All these changes may have occurred in the interest of improving results, but over a period of time this group effort has tugged and yanked at the control, effectively warping it so that it bears little resemblance to the original package.

Rather than asking this patched-up mess to continue as the standard bearer, take a long look at it. Give a creative team a special assignment: Analyze the original package and isolate, if possible, the reasons for its initial success—and then give it new life, instead of just a cosmetic adjustment.

Some of the questions that should be answered include:

- Why did this package beat test after test over a long period of time?
- What sparked its long reign of success? Was it a brilliant articulation of the offer? A powerful graphic idea? A letter that evoked a certain vision? An effective envelope legend? A harmony of colors, graphics, stock, and typeface?

Some ideas do deserve to be abandoned. There are themes, offers, concepts, and propositions that are as dated as a slang phrase. And there are packages that simply are old-fashioned, relics of another marketing era. Nothing will ever bring them back.

But sometimes there's a latent proposition, a big idea that merely has to be freshened. Letting new creative minds rebuild the control is more than just an exercise in nostalgia, it's a return to the source of the power that gave energy to the control in the first place.

In a three-way test, pit the newly designed package against the old control and a new test. See if it doesn't come out first, and the old control second. Then it will really be time to give that old patchwork package an honorable retirement.

Taking "Hidden" Factors Into Account

On the surface, direct marketing appears to be a nice, sensible way of moving products or services. All you need do is observe a couple of not very complicated principles that have worked for thousands before you, and you can bank the results. Your mailing should do well. Your ad will be profitable. Your venture ought to be an accountant's delight.

But something went wrong, and you find yourself with a direct marketing project sadly in need of repair. How can you improve a mailing when you've done the very best possible? How can that ad or commercial be bettered? What should you do to enhance your bottom line?

Well, remember that things are seldom what they seem. There may be hidden factors that you've failed to take into account.

• *Hidden costs.* Did the long-term cost of your project climb much higher than you had estimated? Perhaps you didn't take into account the serious losses that can result from customers failing to renew or reorder, or from cancellations. A realistic assessment of "the second act" of the mail order drama can pay dividends. (The first act is successfully acquiring names through a short-term trial or premium offer. The second act is converting these bargain hunters to full-length subscribers or power buyers.)

Another hidden cost that can ruin the plans of a new book club or book continuity program is the cost of money. The careful plans you've laid down in year no. 1 for year no. 3 of your book club or long-term continuity offer can be destroyed if you haven't factored in debt service on loans to start your enterprise and to keep it going. You've spent your promotional money up front, but revenue collections will be over several years; this is in contrast to a one-shot sale that produces big gobs of revenue almost immediately with no long-term interest pangs. Money to pay interest has to come from somewhere, so prepare to practice good money management at the very outset by watching expenses and shaving unnecessary costs.

• *Hidden lead-analysis factors.* Are you unnecessarily taxing yourself by judging the cost effectiveness of an ad by its open rate, rather than a contract rate you may have earned? Watch your cost per lead drop when you apply the lower rate! Are you being too stringent by not factoring in white mail? If, during the course of a campaign, you suddenly receive a heavy number of leads to which you can't assign a key, look for a mailing that may have been sent out without a return envelope, an ad that lost its key code, or a telephone extension that was never given in the course of a live radio spot. Alert your office staff to be on the lookout for unexplained white mail. Or study your responses to locate strangely weak lists or media, and see if you can't give that white mail a home.

Are you unfairly penalizing an ad that may have run on a national holiday when nobody was clipping coupons, or a mailing that landed in mailboxes during an economic downturn, or a radio spot that was broadcast at the same time as a heavily promoted TV show? Don't think of your promotions as existing in a vacuum.

• *Hidden tonality shortcomings.* Did your copy strike the wrong note with your audience? Did you match your language with your audience? Is the presentation too "showy" for the product or the market? Did you use a hard-to-read typeface in an ad aimed at senior citizens? Did your Spanish-language commercial delivered by a Cuban announcer air on a Puerto Rican station? Was your fund-raising package too slick and professional, too expensive?

• *Hidden media mistakes.* Was your coupon ad backed by another coupon ad? Did you run a mail order coupon ad in a glossy periodical that is treasured and saved—and never clipped? Did your radio spot run only during drive time, when copying down the phone number may mean traffic havoc? Did your two-minute spot interrupt a great movie, instead of providing relief during a bad one?

While you can't control everything concerned with a direct marketing effort, you ought to be aware of those hidden things that live in shadows and come back to haunt even the most buttoned-down direct marketers.

CHAPTER 8

Improve Your Job,
Enhance Your Career

Putting Direct Marketing on the
Organizational Map

Not too long ago, a woebegone figure inhabited a small office in many major business organizations, isolated and ignored—the direct marketing specialist, somebody to be called on only when a sales manager needed a letter written or when a catalog had to be put together. Rarely admitted to strategy meetings and never consulted when it came time to plan the year's sales objectives, the direct marketer, while not exactly a pariah, did not occupy a very high place in the corporate table of organization.

Today, that's all changed. The direct marketing specialist has become very important. Meetings of the board of directors are halted, while the latest mailing is passed around the conference table; and a coupon ad is treated with the respect formerly given a four-color, twelve-page magazine insert.

Management has belatedly discovered what we have known all along—direct marketing is one of the most efficient tools an organization can have. But along with this belated recognition, we have inherited outdated organizational ways of doing business. For all its contributions, the direct marketing department is still being treated like a corporate afterthought.

What is needed is a new configuration that recognizes the status of direct marketing as a key sales and marketing function. That configuation should be built around these structural principles.

1. *Management should have a systemic view of direct marketing.* The organization should be conceived of as a total marketing system, with direct marketing as the linchpin. The direct marketing department should not be isolated; it should be central to planning and execution.

2. *Direct marketing must occupy a more important role in company planning and policy-making.* If a direct marketing manager occupies a place in the table of organization somewhere below the grounds keeper, an organization can't expect good performance. Direct marketing functions must be treated as an essential part of the total marketing plan. The direct marketer should report directly to the chief operating executive, not to the advertising manager, marketing manager, sales promotion manager, or sales manager.

3. *Authority as well as responsibility should be given to the direct marketer.* Why should the approval of the president or treasurer or sales manager be required for *all* direct marketing action? This is often a remnant of the days when direct marketing was a sales-promotion function. But part of a direct marketer's contribution to a company's growth is a quick response to opportunity. To weigh everything down with old-fashioned procedures is to hamper the entrepreneurial spirit of a good direct marketer. If there are lines to be drawn, the role of the direct marketer should be clearly defined

and duties delegated without abject reliance on rubber stamps and the approval of unqualified superiors.

4. *Direct marketing strategy should be integrated into the total marketing and sales plan.* Again and again, a superb direct marketing effort has been wasted because not everybody knew of it. A powerful lead-generating campaign is wasted because the phone operators didn't know how to handle the flood of inquiries. An otherwise effective sales campaign actually loses business when orders can't be filled because of low inventory. Direct marketing touches every part of a company, and should be recognized as an integral part of the common effort to reach common goals.

5. *Direct marketing should be concentrated rather than dissipated.* Because direct marketers employ skills that combine advertising, sales promotion, marketing, and even sales management, they're frequently called upon to put out fires and solve problems in the advertising department or sales promotion unit. The result isn't more kudos for direct marketing. Virtue isn't rewarded. What does happen is that direct marketers lose their identities as specialists and become known as generalists, people with roving commissions, substitute teachers. The department loses its individuality and becomes a picnic basket, where every other department pulls out a goody as wanted. Budgets are then rewritten and direct marketing allocations are awarded to other departments because of the imbalance of personnel. And a once-healthy direct marketing unit fades away, the victim of its own ability.

6. *Direct marketing should be held accountable.* Treating direct marketers as a species of eccentric number crunchers and paper folders results in a curious state of affairs where the direct marketing department becomes a one-night stand rather than a long-running show. Direct marketers may be quite skilled at measuring results of an individual campaign but fall down when it comes to selling the contributions of direct marketing to an overall sales and marketing objective. When there is no built-in measuring system, management can't appreciate the specific achievements of direct marketing. Direct marketers must keep reselling direct marketing to manage-

ment, and must constantly integrate direct market successes within the framework of organizational goals.

The corporate direct marketer cannot inhabit a mountaintop or burrow quietly at the end of a quiet corridor. Getting a good seat at the table of organization requires pushing and shoving and even shouting. While the mailroom may be a traditional route to the top, executive suites will continue to lack a direct mail office until direct marketing specialists ask for the order.

Maverick Direct Marketers

Something interesting has been happening to direct marketing. Perhaps because of the increasing importance of our field, we've been seeing a new breed coming in and making waves.

Not content with doing things the old way "because they always work," they've been asking questions. Why should we be content with a 2.5 percent response, the equivalent of a 97.5 percent failure rate? Why should we use the U.S. Postal Service when electronic media can do the job faster and more dramatically? Why should a direct mail package look like junk? Why should a mail order ad weigh in at 750 words of copy when so many persuasive general ads do the job in only 100 words? Why should a direct response TV commercial be four times as long as other commercials, with execrable production standards to boot? Why can't radio be used to better advantage? Why can't we use research, psychosociology, and psychoeconomics? Just how effective is a brochure enclosure? Why should personalization be repeated eight or nine times in the course of the mailing? Why can't offers be prompted by the customer's needs rather than the mailer's? Why can't copywriters and art directors be team players instead of adversaries? Why call in the production manager after the job has been designed and ask her to rescue you from an impossible format?

Different, risk-taking, impatient, disrespectful, and demanding, the maverick direct marketer has somehow slipped through the organizational defenses of interviews, training programs, and time-encrusted methods, and has begun to mount guerrilla activity in the midst of tried-and-true methodology.

These double agents are not especially interested in remaining in one place forever. They want the opportunity to do important things well, they use words like *integrity* and *ethics*, and they say no more often than yes.

In spite of all the barriers to keep them out—nepotism and cronyism, overwhelming paperwork, interminable conferences, antediluvian procedures, a half nelson on all creativity, and a refusal to acknowledge contributions—these mavericks have used their skills and resources to establish a beachhead and are making their presence known.

Because of the paucity of art directors trained in direct response, more art directors with a background in general advertising are being hired. Impatient with crowded formats hallowed by time, they are producing layouts that are clean and crisp. They're refusing to salt and pepper ads with six or seven typefaces. They won't use typefaces that had their vogue in the 1930s. They won't sit still for cumbersome, wordy headlines that parrot other cumbersome, wordy headlines. And they insist on working closely with copywriters in "creative teams."

Maverick copywriters are not wedded to the word *free* in a headline. They believe it's no longer necessary to tell, and repeat, and repeat once more, in order to sell. They're bringing in techniques and ideas from other media, especially film and television: humor, emotive expressions, flair, and imagination. This cross-pollination is sharpening the look and feel of direct response and bringing it closer to the mainstream of general marketing. (Conversely, the techniques of direct marketing are being adopted by general advertising. No longer is it necessary to come up with just a slogan and a pun and then take a well-earned break. Copywriters are digging into the product and the market and writing copy that is more benefit oriented.)

The mavericks are to be found not only in the creative end of the business. Account executives are creating marketing strategy instead of taking orders from clients. Advertising managers are demanding their agencies deliver more than a paraphrase of last year's advertising. List brokers are exploring new concepts in social and geographic dynamics and using computers to build new combinations and permutations. And entrepreneurs are anticipating market trends, creating new products and services, and making them pay off sooner to the tune of larger profits.

When you examine the history of direct marketing, it becomes evident that the mavericks are the ones who actually have built our discipline, from the mail order geniuses in turn-of-the-century Chicago to the book club inventors of the 1920s to the most recent catalog and telemarketing innovators.

Their impatience, goal-driven perspective, and risk taking sometimes make them poor company. But they are the ones who will take the rest of us—digging in our heels to the bitter end—over the top.

Eleven Principles for Hiring Direct Marketing Freelancers

Sooner or later, you may find that you have to go outside your organization for direct marketing assistance: copy, art, production, broadcast, media, and so forth. There aren't enough good people in direct marketing to go around, so using freelancers is quite routine.

English business writer Antony Jay, in *The Harvard Business Review* (August 1977), noted that, to benefit from the skills of outside people, you need not be an expert yourself but you should be an expert in making good use of their talents. The decision to use freelance help should not be a last-minute one. You're hiring an architect, not a firefighter. So make room on your planning agenda for freelance help early in the game, and use these eleven principles, based on Mr. Jay's ideas, to guide you.

1. *The ask-around principle.* Samples will give an indication of the freelancer's ability, but each project has its own ground rules and conditions, so don't rely too heavily on these. Involve anyone else from your organization in the selection process who will have to work with the freelancer. Check colleagues, friends, organiza-

tions, and publications; also suppliers, printers, and lettershops. *Question to ask:* "Does the freelancer I'm considering consistently bring fresh solutions and innovative ideas to assignments?"

2. *The same-league principle.* Your ego may be massaged by going to the superstars, the biggest and most expensive freelancers, but can your budget afford it? You'll be surprised at the fine quality and results you can get from one of the many lesser lights in the field. *Question to ask:* "Will my project get the priority and involvement it deserves?"

3. *The same-business principle.* While any skilled freelancer can probably market both shoes and sugar, you'll save indoctrination time if you find somebody who's knowledgeable about your business. If you'd like to try a newcomer, give him a little piece of the action. A copywriter might work on a test package, for instance. Just don't throw a vital project at a first-timer. Test him, just as you would test any other component in the mailing itself. An extra bonus when you work with somebody with experience in your area: she may have a different point of view based on knowledge. (William Wrigley once said: "When two people in the same organization agree, one of them is not needed.") *Question to ask:* "Ever come across this problem before?" While no professional freelancer will divulge trade secrets, there is apt to be a vast body of experience to draw upon.

4. *The vanishing-act principle.* Will you sign up some very impressive expert, only to find you're working with his relatively inexperienced and inadequately supervised underlings? That's like arranging for your portrait to be painted by a master, then discovering yourself posing for one of his apprentices. Make sure that what you see is what you're going to get. But don't be surprised if the Great Man doesn't seem to take a great interest in your work. His contributions may be more of an advisory nature, where all he does is sniff the pot and proclaim the dish fit to serve. *Question to ask:* "Where's the boss?"

5. *The don't-tell-me-about-yourself, tell-me-about-myself principle.* The wonderful references, excellent samples, and brilliant record can always be checked out later. Does the freelancer respond to you when you state your needs? Is he paying attention? Or is he mentally drumming his fingers on the table waiting for you to pause so that he can start up his sales spiel again? Or is he busy taking calls? (Some freelancers insist on using their client's office as an extension of their own, even having calls forwarded from other clients and conducting their business on your time.) *Question to ask:* "What did I just say?"

6. *The letter-of-agreement principle.* When you come to terms, ask your freelancer for a brief letter outlining the assignment as he sees it. The letter should include the objectives you've mutually agreed on, as well as the strategy, timing, degree of completion, a noncompetitive work clause, if you feel it's necessary, and payment. *Question to ask:* "Do you understand the assignment?"

7. *The don't-do-it-all-yourself principle.* If you meddle with the judgments and execution of the freelancer, you're not getting what you've paid for. Extensive rewriting, redesigning, and second-guessing are wasteful. If you're unhappy with the freelancer's performance, speak up early. *Question to ask:* "May I make a suggestion?"

8. *The one-big-team principle.* Tell your staff exactly why you're bringing in a freelancer. Insist on their working together. Some clients prefer to have the freelancer work on the premises; others may have no room. (State laws regulating workers' compensation and insurance may also play a part in this decision.) However, use of creative teams—a writer and art director—virtually dictates on-premises activity. If one half of the creative team is a freelancer, make sure the other half doesn't attempt to dominate creative thinking as the resident genius. If you bring in a freelance creative team, reassure your permanent people that their jobs are safe and you're not testing a new crew. Since most creative people have had freelance experience, this temporary arrangement should not seem threatening. However, the ideas and know-how a freelancer brings

to an assignment are permanent acquisitions, which he will leave behind to be used in later projects by your people. *Question to ask:* "Are you a team player?"

9. *The don't-give-up-the-tiller principle.* Remain firmly in charge. Don't walk away from the job, if at all possible. If you have to leave the office for any length of time, make sure you or an assistant can keep in touch with the work. Build review benchmarks into any long-term project so that you can measure progress. *Question to ask:* "How's it going?"

10. *The I-like-it principle.* If the work is good, say so. Freelancers work in a lonely environment. They drift from one project to another. They crave praise and appreciation. And you'll get better value for your money from an enthusiastic worker. *Question to ask:* "Is your work always this great?"

11. *The how-much-is-that-doggy-in-the-window principle.* Bring out the question of compensation at the very first meeting. Tell the freelancer what your budget constraints are. Determine whether you'll pay per project, on an hourly rate, or on a long-term consultation basis. Don't be afraid to get quotes from other sources. Pay promptly, and include several samples of the finished product with your check. *Question to ask:* "How much?"

Treating freelancers as professionals can result in a mutually beneficial arrangement, with both parties satisfied and eager to work together again in the future.

Should You Hire a Direct Marketing Consultant?

The proliferation of direct marketing consultants is one of the latter-day miracles of our business. Put it down to the lack of fully trained personnel or to the mega expansion of direct marketing, but suddenly consultants are seen in the halls of the most important advertising agencies and direct marketing companies, places where, once upon a time, they were as rare as blotter manufacturers at a ballpoint pen convention.

Today, freelance copywriters, list brokers, TV producers, or sweepstakes specialists can call themselves a consultant and add 10 percent to the invoice for the added cachet. But even in the freewheeling atmosphere of direct marketing, consultants can play an important role as pollinators.

Direct marketing consultants are taken on by companies for one or more of these reasons: for the benefit of their expertise, to save money (either on payroll expenses or through the expertise the consultant offers), to provide an independent outlook and an objective alternative to staff thinking, and to supplement staff capability, especially on tight deadlines.

A consultant's cost is usually less than the salaries and benefits paid to full-time specialists. For the small company this can seem to be a blessing, so much so that there are firms with only consultants and no salaried personnel.

However, total reliance on freelance help, temporary workers, and consultants carries with it seeds of a permanent dwarfing of an enterprise. In-house development is inhibited. A staff of loyal, devoted employees is never put together. And don't forget that consultants, in order to prosper, are forced to leave and go to the next assignment once they've finished their job. Lack of continuity is one of the most important arguments against depending entirely on consultants.

But what about the occasional use of consultants? Using direct marketing consultants can mean the profitable leasing of an outside, objective viewpoint. Often consultants can be decisive where company executives are not. Not tied down to any company position, consultants can slash through an obviously political idea. They have more credibility than management figures with axes to grind. And, theoretically, consultants are above party politics, since they aren't—or shouldn't be—after the presidency or advertising manager's job.

But consultants don't want to merely advise and consent. They want long-term contracts, and that means wooing the people in power. So, all too often, you will find a consultant siding with the most powerful elements in the department rather than exercising objective, rational, intellectual judgment. The consultant will attack certain stances and creative positions, knowing full well that these exposed possibilities (probably expendable to begin with) are just a handful of the alternatives offered. The consultant has saved face, has proved to be a professional, and has kept important friendships going—all the while maintaining a semblance of disinterest and independence.

Putting consultants to work and putting their ideas to work are two different things. Often a direct marketing consultant is frantically hired as a last resort. Promises have been made to management or a client and the day of reckoning is nigh.

Some think the very act of hiring a consultant is the equivalent of solving the problem. Of course, this is not so. You have to put the consultant's ideas to work as well. And if you're not ready to accept the solutions of the consultant, if you feel that some outsider can't really help you or you can't sell the ideas to your boss, then you don't want a consultant's special suggestions or thoughtful breakthroughs. You want a full-time miracle worker who will walk on water without competing with you. You had better reexamine the problem, redefine it, and hope it might just go away. (No direct marketing consultant can be effective in a situation where the client is unable to express his needs or put the recommendations to work.)

Well, how best to use a consultant? The most productive use of a consultant's time is as a gadfly, a pest who will question your judgment rather than endorse it. Ask the consultant to examine your decisions. Experienced consultants may have come across a better mousetrap elsewhere. Or, unfettered by politics or the usual managerial obligations, they can use quantum leaps of imagination and apply a solution used by another client to your dissimilar problem.

When choosing a consultant, look for the anecdotalist, the repository of case studies. Allowing for discretion and confidentiality, the experienced direct marketer consultant builds a body of expertise and know-how to be successfully applied against each new client's needs. You can well benefit from other companies who have been in a similar situation, thanks to the connection offered by the wandering direct marketing consultant, the Johnny Appleseed of our industry.

Are You a Direct Marketing Pro?

One of the most exciting developments in our business has been the outpouring of seminars, lectures, courses, and academic programs devoted to direct marketing. We are seeing a pragmatic business change into a field worthy of study on the theoretical level.

While we have all bandied around the term *direct marketing professional* for years, perhaps it's time to really analyze it, and to decide whether we are on the way to becoming a profession and are qualified to bear the title "professional direct marketer." (Judging from the experiences in other areas, there is apt to be a rivalry between those calling themselves Certified Direct Marketers and those designated Professional Direct Marketers.)

Just what is a profession? Generally speaking, it's a livelihood with a status higher than a trade or craft. But there are definite characteristics marking a profession, and most observers agree that these characteristics are divided into the following attitudinal and structural qualities.

ATTITUDINAL QUALITIES

1. *Collegial.* You are judged by your colleagues and peers on your merits and qualifications.

2. *Public service value.* While many professions deal with people in special states of need, some, such as architecture and engineering, are not primarily service oriented. However, members of all professions are expected to devote a certain amount of time to public service in one way or another.

3. *Self-regulation.* Governed from within, the profession has a regulatory body set up as a quasilegal organization, such as a bar association or medical society, which may be answerable to governmental authority.

4. *Sense of calling.* Because of the long training required or because of the nature of the profession, a strong motivation is necessary.

5. *Autonomy.* One may work either as an individual practitioner or as a member of a group, depending on the profession. Consultants, experts, and specialists have roles to play in the profession.

6. *Earned rewards.* Because of the specialized knowledge, training, and usefulness of the profession, society generally acknowledges that professionals should be well paid. Teachers, librarians, nurses, and the clergy are obvious exceptions.

STRUCTURAL QUALITIES

1. *Full-time occupation with specialized knowledge.* Professionals are employed in their profession full-time. The knowledge and skills have been acquired during a prolonged period of education and training. Many professions require a minimum of two years of college-level training; others call for graduate school internships and continuing education throughout one's career. In the tradition of the three "learned" professions—medicine, law, and divinity— there is emphasis on study, scholarship, and contribution to the body of knowledge of the profession through papers, monographs, publications, speeches, and activity in professional groups.

2. *Training schools.* Supervised by professional associations, training schools may be independent bodies or affiliated with universities. In addition, these schools usually have publishing and research facilities, because they have the responsibility of codifying professional knowledge.

3. *Professional association.* Professional credentials are issued by the association, which defines competency.

4. *Licensing or certification and community recognition.* Often armed with quasi-governmental authority, the professional association sets standards for licensing and certification. These standards

are accepted by the public as the only means of judging a professional.

5. *Code of ethics.* The level of work must be in the best interest of the client and of the community at large. Standards, confidentiality, and an understanding of the needs of the client are part of any professional-client relationship.

6. *Decision making, using an established body of knowledge.* Principles, theories, and propositions that have been tested and found to be true are used in the exercise of judgment. Even the most innovative professional has a firm grip on the established and familiar, moving then to the different and the ground-breaking. A keen sense of precedent and empiricism is part of the professional method.

7. A *sense of responsibility.* This includes pride in one's work, devotion to it, and the duty to produce the finest work possible. Sometimes called "professionalism."

Using these benchmarks, can you call yourself a direct marketing professional? Can direct marketing call itself a profession? Or do we still have a long way to go?

What Is a Direct Marketing Communicator?

Who calls the tune in direct marketing? The mailer or advertiser? The agency? The outside consultant?

Years ago, the answer was fairly simple: "He who pays the piper calls the tune." The hand that signed the checks and the letters often wrote the copy and initialed the purchase orders. But as direct marketing became more sophisticated, more technical, more costly, we started seeing a special person making the decisions: the *direct marketing communicator.* Sometimes this could be a writer, sometimes an account executive or a list specialist, and, of course, sometimes the president or vice-president in charge of everything.

The direct marketing communicator sets the tone of the promotion, campaign, ad, or mailing, molds the concept, and selects the path along which the advertising must go. As the final arbiter of media and lists, the editor of copy, the critic of graphics, and the judge of quality, the direct marketing communicator has a tremendous responsibility. And because more good direct marketing is being produced by a collective mind, the total experience and judgment of a whole slew of experts, the communicator's job is to balance the forces within this group. Because the focus is so often on the characteristics of this collective rather than on the abilities of one person, the skills of a host of people are called for, working together in a social situation with its own strains and conflicts, aims and problems. Throughout all this, the communicator must juggle sensitivities, budgetary constraints, immediate sales objectives, and long-term goals.

A look at the social structure of a direct marketing department or agency can be quite revealing. Roles are now blurred by virtue of the ambiguities in the distinction between responsibilities. A writer may design a package; an account executive rewrites the letter; a client selects a mailing list; a production manager vetoes a paper stock; an art director writes a headline.

So we see that participants in the direct marketing effort are attacked by various pressures, including financial and creative expectations. Too often the solution is willy-nilly compromise, a committee decision satisfactory to nobody, or an executive veto that leaves everybody frustrated.

Enter the direct marketing communicator, the crucial function that links specializations. The direct marketing communicator has to resolve conflicts, balance creative and marketing goals, and integrate everything within the constraints of budgets and time.

The job is not easy. If the communicator plays too heavy a role in the creative process, he may find himself either a "creative participant" or an "interfering parasite." Outside his own specialty, if he has one, he may make some costly technical error. He may misread the market, not quite understand the product or service, or ignore political forces within the organization that could bring him to his knees.

For instance, writers and art directors often believe that they are being exploited, while management is convinced that they are valued but overpaid prima donnas. Specialists such as list managers, production managers, and the like are protected by their very skills but feel they are not appreciated. Clients respect the expertise of agencies or consultants, but have definite ideas on direction, objectives, and execution. Suppliers must juggle customers, the possibility of future assignments, and limited time and resources.

In all, the direct marketing structure has a number of built-in instabilities and conflicts that must be resolved if a mailing, ad, or commercial is to be produced. Putting the bits and pieces together is the task of the communicator, who has to unify the elements of the promotion, the requirements of the customer, who is paying for everything, the legal and ethical standards, production and creative values, and the goal of achieving a low cost per order or beating the control or introducing a new product.

How is all this achieved? Sociologists examining complex organizations such as a direct marketing department have found that there's a control structure that gets things done: a balance of power and authority, where participants understand that the exercise of authority is the exercise of legitimate power; the boss is boss because he's the boss. Other observers have noted the adroit manipulation of a shared belief: "We're trying to reach the same goal: direct mail that works."

The direct marketing communicator does wield power, but realizes that harnessing a variety of creative talents calls for mutual satisfaction and a total commitment by everybody concerned, and so treads carefully through this mine field of personalities, priorities, and private ambitions.

Direct marketing is a communication system involving a receiver (prospect), a medium (mail, print, broadcast, telemarketing), and a communicator (the direct marketing producer-director-catalyst-organizer-sparkplug-general-judge). To make sure the receiver gets the message by way of the medium is the job of the direct marketing communicator—no longer a writer or advertising bigwig but a "connector," the gatekeeper allowing only the best and strongest ideas into the marketplace.

Your Creative Clock: How to Keep Track

Whenever a copywriter is asked, "How much time do you think you'll need for this job?" he or she actually has a choice of five modes for an answer.

1. *The facetious mode.* "How much time do you want me to have?" can be the quick-as-the-flash retort. After the initial burst of shared hilarity, the questioner goes off to call up headhunters, looking for a replacement.

The facetious mode isn't the answer.

2. *The financial mode.* This is also the mercenary or venial mode. Usually limited to freelancers, who suddenly discover how valuable their time can be. A two-page letter assumes the importance of the Gettysburg Address. A full-page ad rivals *Ulysses.* And a thirty-second radio spot may take Eugene O'Neill, oh, a very long time to write.

This is also a favorite ploy of overworked agency writers, who are faced with a mighty full plate or who loathe the client or the account executive or the chore. And so a simple two-hour job becomes a full day's exercise.

3. *The factual mode.* The novice sits down with a calculator and figures out her typing speed and necessary pauses for inspiration. And sadly underestimates the time needed.

4. *The fantastic or figurative mode.* Nobody really takes this number seriously. It's used to pad an estimate or fill out a required form.

5. *The faithful mode.* Sometimes called "experiential." Still used by honest professionals, who take into consideration necessary interplay with other people, jobs down the pike, and what has occurred before.

Well, how *do* you estimate how long a creative assignment will take? By keeping a time log, so you can learn how to apportion your time most profitably.

Start by writing down the jobs that you have to perform each day and how long you think they'll take. Then keep a fifteen-minute activity record. Log phone calls, five-minute breaks, proofreading assignments, everything. Do this for at least a week. Then compare your actual time with the rough estimate. There will be substantial differences between how you thought your time would be spent and how you actually spent it.

Now enter the actual number of minutes in a permanent record. So the next time someone asks you how long you will spend writing a two-page collection letter, or conceptualizing a two-minute commercial, or building a full-page ad, you'll know!

The important thing to remember is that every creative person has a different clock. And you shouldn't be judged by another person's output.

Industrial engineers measure the times used for various elements of the job by applying correction factors and by making allowances for personal time, delays, and fatigue. But they rarely take into consideration decisions involving discretion and judgment.

If you're a supervisor, you know what you can expect a writer to turn out during a certain period and you ought to be able to demand reasonable performance requirements. But this comes with observation during average conditions. You can't expect creative people to turn out work at top speed and you shouldn't make promises to account management or to clients that can't be fulfilled.

The empirical discipline we bring to judging the results of a mailing may well be used in estimated hours needed to complete a job. Rely on experience. Keep careful records. And allow for the human factor. It'll help you to make a timely estimate that you won't have to apologize for later on.

Why It Pays to Keep a Career Log

As any Trekkie can attest, it was a fortunate thing for TV's *Star Trek* that James Kirk was required to keep a captain's log, otherwise there would have been no plot or narrative.

To a sailor, a log is a diary of a voyage. This marine journal contains vital information, such as course, leeway, direction and force of the wind, speed, state of the weather, and other subjects of importance. And in admiralty court or insurance investigations, for instance, it can be an essential piece of evidence.

In recent years, the professional logbook has become a tool in business. It works much like a nautical logbook, as a journal of noteworthy activities and incidents. However, it's kept by an individual as a record of genuine achievements on the job, however modest they may seem. In a record-keeping and numbers-heavy area like direct marketing, this logbook can perform at least three vital functions.

1. *Job diary.* If your organization uses formal periodic performance appraisals, here's a way to tip the scales to your benefit. Even the most benevolent management tends to forget or overlook an individual employee's contributions, but they never forget mistakes. Keep your own independent record of your accomplishments, and keep it on a weekly basis. Did you do a particularly good job on a certain mailing? Put down the specifics—percentage of return, savings realized, kudos from the client, and so on. Did you contribute any good ideas in a meeting? List them in your journal, even though they may never have been used.

With the exception of ego-bruising confrontations over raises, promotions, or extra time off, some managers are never quite able to communicate dissatisfaction or incompatibility. However, with this record, you can regularly evaluate your impressions of your boss's feelings about your work (be careful, though, not to let this effort turn into a litany of paranoic perceptions). Are you getting the recognition you deserve? Is there a pattern of not acknowledging your work? (Many managers are too busy or, surprisingly, too shy, to say, "Well done." This record can remind them—and yourself— of your worth.) At review time, use the journal as evidence for your claim to a promotion or raise, or to counter any accusations of being "becalmed or rudderless." Be careful not to confide confidential matters, such as proprietary business affairs, to your job diary, where others may see it.

2. *Career progress report.* How have you advanced professionally? Are you doing a better job today than, say, three years ago? What have you learned? Are you moving ahead of your peers? Falling behind? Be tough on yourself in this personal performance appraisal, but be realistic as well. Set goals that are within your reach. Otherwise, you'll be always tormenting yourself with impossible objectives. Use this benchmark to measure progress and to make sure you're still on course. Again, don't use this as a recital of resentments. When you're writing your résumé, refer to this personal career progress report. It'll be a lot easier to get a fix on your best points if you've been noting them down over the years.

3. *Project analysis.* This is perhaps the most valuable documentation of all. After you've completed an ad, commercial, or mailing, write a memo to yourself. Recap the reasons you chose a particular creative direction or list strategy, and write a paragraph on the competitive environment. Analyze the results. Then in a summary paragraph tell yourself what you may have learned. List the reasons you would repeat this particular strategy, or why you would do things differently next time.

The ancient mariners who sailed where no man had sailed before devised charts, so that those who came after them would not encounter the same hazards and difficulties. You should keep a record of your creative journeys, so that you can learn from them and return to them, even years later, for ideas or inspiration.

Starting Up a Newsletter

After looking over the titles of the thousand or so newsletters in the *Ayer's Directory of Publications* (a fraction, incidentally, of the thousands of newsletters published around the world, unheralded, unsung, and, alas, often unread), a thoughtful observer might be tempted to note that newsletters are the harvest of direct marketers' daydreams being nurtured by moonlight.

In other words, it is the rare direct marketing writer, art director, account executive, or mail order manager who, especially in this era of desktop publishing, hasn't thought seriously about publishing a newsletter: that unique small business that you're supposed to be able to operate in your spare time, without employees and with very little capital.

There is, however, a serpent or two in this vision of paradise. Very often newsletter ideas are hatched as desperate reactions to job frustration, early retirement, boredom, second-career yearnings, or the need for additional income. A marketing plan has never been worked up. Basic questions such as adequate capitalization, publication schedules, design, printing and distribution, routine clerical and bookkeeping operations, and a steady flow of stories have been ignored or shrugged aside. And to top it off, the all-important entrepreneurial spark, commitment, and willingness to take a chance may be missing. So many a daydreaming moonlighter winds up the morning after with nothing to show for it but a great big headache.

However, let's assume that almost all the ingredients for launching and running a successful newsletter are in place. One component is missing: the Big Idea. How do you find it? With thousands of newsletters already being published, how do you identify a market, a need, prospects within the market, and the hot buttons that would appeal to prospects?

One technique is the "look at the lists" method. Just go through SRDS's *Direct Mail List Directory* or flip through the cards of your neighborhood list broker. The brief descriptions of each list can sometimes spark a newsletter idea.

For instance, in going through the various categories of lists, you discover that there are 37,000 retail jewelry establishments in the United States. What if you offered them a newsletter on using direct marketing to promote their stores? What about a newsletter on travel ideas to the 100,000 members of the Travel America Club? A budget recipe newsletter to the 146,000 parents who sent in Franco American Spaghettios coupons? A newsletter on car restoration to 104,000 car book buyers?

Just what would the newsletter be about? Instead of idly drawing up editorial plans, write a sales letter. "Blue sky" the contents; that is, describe the newsletter in hardhitting promotional language, with benefits and specifics. By the time you have completed your letter, you will have a very good idea of what the newsletter should be about. Then go back and tone down your language and promises for the actual mailing!

Incidentally, this technique of writing the promotional material *first* was originally used in creating self-help books, at a time when FTC and postal regulations were more casual. (It was also used by business promoters writing prospectuses before the days of the SEC!) The copywriter was charged with the task of coming up with a new book idea or modifying an aging one. He would design a table of contents and then write a sales letter around it. If the book idea received management's approval, a freelance writer would be given the assignment to create a book. Sometimes, the verdict of the marketplace was needed, and only after a good response was received from a mailing would the book ever see the light of day. (Today, the postal service looks askance at mailers who offer what they don't have.)

Now it's time to show your mettle. The money you would have used for your vacation, driveway repairs, or your parakeet's orthodontia work has to go to pay for a test mailing. Forget those out-of-date $200 per 1,000 guidelines. Anyway, small players pay more than the big guys who get volume discounts. Be prepared to discover that list houses and lettershops don't give away their services, that the post office wants money in advance, that there are typography and photography expenses, and tiny little bills that keep popping up like ants at a picnic.

But after all, there's no gain without pain, and you are just dipping a toe in the great big ocean.

If the results to your charter subscription offer warrant it, don't quit your job just yet. This will be a part-time venture for a long, long time, maybe forever. Be prepared to spend some more money, this time with a lot more confidence! Your initial subscription list will not pay the freight. You've probably come up with a short-term introductory offer that enticed the prospective reader, and you will lose money on each new subscriber. You'll have to wait for renewals to begin to make money. But you do have a powerful tool for raising money: your response rate. Assuming your universe is large enough and your rate high enough, simple arithmetic will show prospective investors that you have a promising venture.

But if you've husbanded your resources carefully, there's no need to give up any equity at this stage. Use a local quick-copy shop to run off the few copies of your newsletter. Don't make any investments. Collaters, postage meters, and computerized mailing systems will all come later.

The one commitment you should make is in keeping your contract with your subscribers. Stop eating lunch and start reading trade publications. Invest in stringers, expert correspondents with special expertise in your newsletter's subject. Spend weekends keeping your subscription lists current and billing subscribers. Write renewal series until you get one that works. Publish on a regular basis. Forget bowling night. Sell your TV. And be prepared to run a regular post office or lettershop schedule. And when your boss looks crooked at you, think of that character in *The Threepenny Opera* who dreams of the day when a ship's cannon will blast all her enemies away. You've put down your down payment on *your* ship coming in some day.

And don't be discouraged if, after all those moonlit hours, your newsletter doesn't get off the ground. For every successful Willard Kiplinger's *Washington Letter*, there is an unsuccessful Craig Claiborne *Restaurant Letter*. And even Time Inc. has yet to discover a formula that consistently brings magazine ideas to life. Don't just dream in the moonlight, use your dreaming as a photosynthetic force to nurture and grow your hopes.

How to Spot the Creative Individual

If you had to recruit somebody for a creative position, what would you look for?

Here's a useful compendium of five major creative characteristics you can use as litmus paper the next time you're told a person is "creative." *Warning:* These attributes are arbitrary and would probably flunk a Thematic Apperception Test.

1. *The creative person is fluent*, able to produce a staggering number of ideas very quickly. Ask a creative art director for a new ad format and you'll get four. Turn to a creative account executive

for some new marketing strategies and you'll get a fourteen-page memo. This conceptual fluency can result in an abundance of clever innovations that a stern—and often not very creative—taskmaster must cull.

2. *The creative individual tends to avoid commitment* and hesitates to pass judgment on the do-ability of a new idea, although quite often he is in full command of technique and method. (See no. 5.) He would rather ramble than refine. Again, somebody has to pick up the pieces, but sometimes those pieces can be magnificent! "Paper folders," those talented direct mail designers who "push the envelope outward," have forced new technology on our business. They go where no man has ever gone before—and lasers and ink-jetting and whacky formats follow.

3. *The creative person is egotistical,* choosing and pursuing problems without too much interest in policy or planning. This free-form exploration should be encouraged, and "what-iffers" ought to be given their head. That's where you get the mailing lists chosen because somebody has a hunch that pays off. The screwy media buy that results in a lower cost per order than ever dreamed of before. The production technique that nobody would touch, until some "dreamer" bulldozes it through successfully.

4. *The creative person takes risks.* The copywriter who takes chances and won't give fourteen reasons why and the art director who insists that a coupon need not have a dotted border can infuriate the most mild-mannered of advertising managers. Until the results come in. While not many crazy ideas pan out, some do—the buck slip, the superscription, the remnant ad—and in the process create their own ethos and methodology for others to follow blindly . . . until another generation of innovators comes along.

5. *The creative person is a dreamer* whose feet are planted firmly on the ground. While blessed (or cursed) with an exuberant imagination and rich associative thinking, the creative individual knows precisely what he is doing. A master technician who is meticulous, almost pedantic about ways and means (the truly creative art director

insists on perfect typography, not slipshod typesetting; the truly creative copywriter reveres language and researches a project with the zeal of an investigative journalist), the innovator does not confuse creative and productive functions.

How to Spot the Creative Organization

What kind of a company would you want to work for? Or want to hire for an assignment?

If you're like most people in direct marketing, you probably would be happiest in a creative organization. But what makes an organization creative? How can you actually define a creative organization? You might start with these five criteria, and from there go on to construct your own template.

1. *The creative organization doesn't try to follow in the footsteps of another company.* Its objectives are original. It may be as different as a book club offering titles exclusively on paperweights or it may be a general book club breaking new ground in offers and premiums. Or it may be a catalog house "bending" ideas—using the negative-option concept to sell flower seeds, for instance.

2. *The creative organization refuses to indulge in cut-and-dried decision making.* While this may lead to a certain looseness in meeting deadlines, it does foster innovation. For instance, a commitment to basic research and contemplation of alternative ways of doing business can break new ground. While many mail order specialists were content to go after the same customers year in and year out, with very little change of product, other companies were borrowing ideas from sociology, economics, and psychology to find new markets. Spiegel, for instance, refused to be a second-tier Sears, and went on to successfully exploit the Yuppie revolution and changes in consumer and credit habits.

3. *The creative organization doesn't evaluate ideas and suggestions depending on the originator.* The junior copywriter who *insists* on rewriting boilerplate (to the confusion and despair of legal

departments) isn't put in her place. Instead, her copy is given a fair test. And the production manager isn't tossed out on his ear just because he offers an apparently revolutionary variation on a brochure layout. Content, not the source, is the touchstone that a creative organization uses to judge an idea. Suggestion boxes and ad hoc surveys are not blackballed simply because they're informal.

4. *The creative organization has developed various procedures for producing ideas very quickly.* These procedures may consist of creativity-stimulation techniques such as brainstorming and synectics, or special commando units made up of people from all divisions who come together to solve a problem, or an open-door policy that welcomes ideas from everybody, including vendors and clients.

5. *The creative organization is a hotbed of new ideas but remains a well-run company.* Consider a well-established university. Blessed with a fine endowment and gifted fund raisers, it is also a home for thinkers, creators, and innovators—while providing a solid education. It may even have a decent football team.

If you can, audit the annual report of a think tank, the research organization that can get away with awesome fees because it produces ideas that make money. Or think about those other wild places: the very expensive design studio that sets new standards in graphics, the movie studio that consistently turns out Oscar winners, the Broadway producers who always have successful shows, the hot advertising agency, the TV production company with several well-rated shows. They all have very wise managers in charge—people who establish controls, security, stability. While they themselves may not be innovative, they can create environments for producing ideas. For it is written, "Blessed are the Philistines for they shall encourage risk taking."

The Direct Marketing Game

Here is a very elementary introduction to *game simulation*, a technique that encourages abstract decision making. The possibilities for its use in direct marketing have yet to be explored. And although this is a simplistic, once-over-lightly view of this experimental form (game-simulation students will note the omission of a chance mechanism, for example), it is hoped that this little experience will lead others to construct scenarios that can really be of assistance in solving problems.

1. An unexpected $16,000 legacy has inspired you to become a first-time mail order entrepreneur. Although your knowledge of the stationery business is minimal, you're convinced that what the world needs now is an expensive fountain pen.

You've heard that the U.S. distributors of a deluxe $200 fountain pen made in Europe are willing to wholesale it at a 50 percent discount in minimum lots of 50, providing you pay cash with order.

Many questions need to be answered before you go into the mail. It's all new to you, and so, without sorting out their priority, you try to address each problem. For instance, should you sell the pen at a discount (go to number 2) or charge list price (go to number 3)?

2. You do a quick "market survey" by checking local newspaper ads, and you find that stationery stores are either selling the pen at list or are discounting it for an average price of $190. Go to number 4.

3. You decide to sell the pen at the nationally advertised price of $200. You want your mailing to have a first-class appearance, and you hire the services of a local printer specializing in engraved invitations. He in turn recommends a high school English teacher as a writer. An art teacher from the same high school is commissioned to design a package. During this intensively creative period, you come across an article on direct mail in a national inspirational magazine and you decide to follow its advice. You call a local advertising agency specializing in promotions to physicians. They quickly locate a list of doctors for you. (After all, physicians write a lot of prescriptions, so they need fancy pens, don't they?)

An engraved invitation is sent to these physicians, offering them the opportunity to buy a $200 pen by mail from a stranger. Unfortunately, the mailing goes out just as stationery stores around the country hold their annual inventory clearance sales. You receive only 125 orders. Go to number 10.

4. You decide to offer the pen at a competitive 15 percent discount, which you feel sure will be lower than prices in most parts of the country. You plan a mail promotion around this $170 offer. Now go to number 5.

5. You plan that the cost of this mailing will be ultimately paid for by your $70 pretax gross profit. Holding on to $6,000 to pay for pens, shipping materials, and overhead, you have $10,000 to spend on this promotion. You plan to fill orders from your basement, using the volunteer services of your wife and two teenage children and the moral support of your dachshund and Siamese cat.

You hope to "bootstrap" subsequent purchases from sales income. Now the question arises: How much should you earmark per package? You've heard somewhere that you can't produce a decent mailing in small quantities for less than $400 per 1,000 names—or was that $1,000 per 400 names? Anyway, without quite knowing the size of the marketplace, you assume that your first drop will be to 25,000 people. Go to number 6.

6. You've constructed a spreadsheet and a what-if scenario. You learn that if your mailing to 25,000 results in a 2 percent pull, you will receive 500 orders, for a gross of $85,000. After buying 500 pens at the wholesale rate of $100 each, and paying $10,000 for a mailing of 25,000 at $400 per 1,000, you will net $25,000. Your spreadsheet also tells you that a 1 percent pull will net you 250 orders. After paying for 250 pens and that $10,000 fixed mailing cost, you will net $7,500. Should you pull out all stops (go to number 7), or should you check your spreadsheet further, and find out that a pull of 0.5 percent will land you 125 orders, for a gross of $21,250 (go to number 8)?

7. After getting bids from freelance copywriters, designers, printers, lettershops, and list houses, you decide to do it yourself, in which case you go to number 9. If you choose to use professional help, go to number 11.

8. Those 125 orders will have to be filled within thirty days or the money returned. You'll have to drive out to the distributor, give him a certified check or cash for $12,500, and load 125 pens in your car. You will also have to buy a rubber stamp, 125 no. 00 Jiffy bags, some blank labels and billheads, and give your horrified children the choice of working in a damp basement for a few days or doing without the newest rock album. You pay $10,000 for the mailing, snap at your wife, step on your dog, kick the cat, bite the bullet, and get out of mail order with a minimum loss of $1,250. (You write off the cost of shipping materials and labor.) You pray that no merchandise will be returned and no checks bounced.

Your adventure ends here.

9. You decide to do it yourself. First you create a mailing package. You write a broadside that announces the offer of a $170 pen, and you have it set in type and printed at a local job-printing shop. You've found a classified ad that offers 25,000 names on gummed labels of people who have bought mail order products, and you send the advertiser $200. You receive a batch of dot-matrix–printed gummed labels, and your "work force" begins to stick them on the printed envelopes you have ordered, after which they fold and insert the broadsides. At the last minute, you order small (no. 6) return envelopes printed with your name and address, and have them inserted as well. Every three days, you stop at the post office for postage stamps, which your crew glues on the envelopes. Finally, after a threat of armed insurrection, you call a halt to the slave labor and mail the 5,000 pieces so far assembled.

You obviously need help, so you contact a small commercial art studio whose sign you've noticed on Main Street, and you virtually dictate the design and copy to them. You leave it to them to produce it, washing your hands of all the problems associated with production. Although they convince you to rent a mailing list, you still want to use at least part of your "bargain" labels. They help to arrange for a mailing permit, and, after a terrific battle, show you the advantages of a business reply envelope over the unstamped blank return envelopes you had proposed to use. Everything is put in the mail. Finally, orders begin to trickle in. You're very disappointed. There are only 125 orders. Go to number 10.

10. Those 125 orders will have to be filled within thirty days or the money returned. You'll have to drive out to the distributor, give him a certified check or cash for $12,500, and load 125 pens in your car. You will also have to buy a rubber stamp, 125 no. 00 Jiffy bags, some blank labels and billheads, and give your horrified children the choice of working in a damp basement for a few days or doing without the newest rock album. You pay $10,000 for the mailing, snap at your wife, step on your dog, kick the cat, bite the bullet, and get out of mail order with a minimum loss of $1,250. (You write off the cost of shipping materials and labor.) You pray that no merchandise will be returned and no checks bounced.

Your adventure ends here.

11. You receive an eloquent fund-raising appeal from your alumni association, and you find yourself responding to the carefully reasoned appeal. You drop a check in the mail, and then decide to call the director of development at your alma mater. "Who wrote that wonderful letter?" you ask. She gives you the name of a professional freelancer. Go to number 12.

12. You call him up and arrange to get together.

He winces at your merchandising scheme, and you wince at the size of his quoted fee. "Brain surgeons don't make that kind of money!" you say. "There are more brain surgeons than there are direct mail copywriters," he retorts.

You strike a deal. In two weeks he returns with a marketing proposition, which includes a discount price offer, a free trial, and a free bottle of ink (retail value $5). He also includes a credit-card payment plan and a one-year guarantee.

"What about copy?"

He promises a draft in two weeks.

Sure enough, in fourteen days he returns with a six-page letter. "This tells me more than I want to know about fountain pens!" you shout. He murmurs something about "not selling without telling."

There's copy for a brochure as well, but he wants to test a portion of the mailing without a brochure. In fact, he uses the word *test* a lot.

He also wants to test the format of the letter: typed versus imitation handwritten versus a handwritten P.S.

By this time, you realize you're in the hands of a maniac. Or a genius. He shows you how to work with an art director. And how to spend money. (Your old budget has been long abandoned.) He also gives you a lesson on how to choose mailing lists, and uses words like *demographics, buying habits,* and *lifestyles.* Go to number 13.

13. You are now completely in his power, so when he recommends a meeting with your pen supplier, you meekly agree. A deal is struck with the distributor for a more equitable discount, and you also find yourself signing a cooperative advertising agreement.

You want to get into the mail immediately, but he cautions you. "Not the right time. Stationery stores are clearing out old merchandise."

He has another surprise for you. You want to mail to 25,000 people. "No," he says. "Let's test 5,000 names." Go to number 14.

14. A small test is mailed. He shows you how to keep track of responses. He explains the mathematics of direct marketing, forecasting, and back-end analysis.

"Is it time?" you ask. By now, he's become your Zen master and Marine Corps drill instructor.

"It is time," he replies. Go to number 15.

15. You call him up. "The responses—I can't handle the orders!"

He counsels you on fulfillment procedures. You hire a fulfillment house. You take a much-needed trip to Hawaii, leaving the dachshund and cat behind to watch the store.

Your adventure ends here. But not before you send him a fountain pen as a gift. He is still waiting for the bottle of ink.

CHAPTER 9

Back to the Future: Classics of Direct Marketing

How to Sell an English Course in Four Pages

The assignment is straightforward. You have to sell a $150 correspondence course by mail to a list of prospects who answered an ad and have received one discount offer to date. Culling out the handful of people who bought on the discount offer, you're faced with a list that is now somewhat aged. How do you go about converting stale inquiries to sales?

This was the problem faced by a copywriter in 1925 whose name has been lost to history. He or she was told to sit at the typewriter and not get up until a good sales letter was written for the Sherwin Cody Course in English. (The price of the course was then $30, but I've multiplied it by five to allow for the sixty-year decline of the dollar.)

Here's what that anonymous copywriter came up with: a four-page letter that is a sparkling example of right-to-the-jugular-vein direct mail copy.

217

Impersonal as a laundry ticket, the letter's salutation is to "Dear Friend," but no friend was ever subjected to this kind of nonstop selling.

I want to remind you that the special $10 Reduction Offer made to you is about to expire; I hope you won't lose this opportunity. [Yes, that's a semicolon, and yes, that's a capitalized O in Offer.]

Since you wrote to us, a fascinating booklet entitled "Mistakes Commonly Made in English" has come from our printer. To make sure you receive a copy of it promptly, I enclose one with this letter.

I feel sure that you will enjoy reading this little book, because your request of a short time ago showed that you are ambitious to increase your success by improving your command of the English language. [Reminding the prospect that he had requested information, and telling him gently what he had asked about.]

You do not need to be told that command of English is the only power on earth which will enable you to get other people to do what you want them to do—and you know well what that means to your greater success. No one denies that the ability to persuade, to convince others by effective spoken and written words, is indispensable to every person who is determined to advance into a worthwhile, highly-paid executive position, or to win friends in the social world. [Class, remember Maslow's hierarchy of needs? We've just seen somebody climb from the base to the very point of the pyramid in three seconds flat. In 1925, there was no neat Lifestyle Indicator to tell the writer to whom he was writing. You had to assume that your reader was the only tenant on Hard Scrabble Road with a Rolls-Royce—in short, it could be anyone.]

This needs no argument; you realize it instinctively. But I wonder if you realize how quickly and easily you can gain the success-compelling powers of eloquent language—through the scientific "short-cut" method now offered you in Sherwin Cody's 100% Self-Correcting Course in English. [The word *short-cut* was first seen in print in the sixteenth century, according to the *Oxford English Dictionary*, but in 1925, it was still considered strange enough to require quotation marks around it. However, the hybrid "success-compelling" was not flagged.]

A few weeks ago I was wondering how to bring home more forcefully to every inquirer the need for Mr. Cody's wonderfully helpful teaching—and suddenly the answer came to me. [A lovely instance of the "page-turner." This is the very last line on page 1 of the letter. Nothing blatant. Not a broken sentence, to be continued on page 2. But an example of the storyteller's art: "What happened next?"]

Why not give all prospective students a list of errors commonly made in English, and let them see for themselves whether they can surely and quickly pick out the correct form every time? Let them see for themselves whether they really know whether the "e" should go before or after the "i"— whether they are sure of their punctuation or not—whether they can decide unhesitatingly between the right and the wrong form. [Taking the reader into your confidence has always proved to be an effective selling method.]

The copywriter goes on to show how Sherwin Cody spent twenty years of tireless experimenting to get rid of old-fashioned methods of teaching English, presumably in much the same way that Edison invented the light bulb or Joseph Aspdin invented Portland cement.

Testimonials are cited. Mrs. Nola Jackson, of Martin, Tennessee, reported, "It is so interesting that one can hardly put it aside until it is finished." Not allowing the reader to doubt this emotional outburst, the copywriter hastens to append this dubious comment:

All the letters received from students express their intense satisfaction with the remarkable progress made, and breathe the spirit of gratitude for the opportunity to take this real "short-cut" method to mastery of English. [Although the FTC was eleven years old by this time, it didn't seem to be concerned with this sort of unprovable statement, which could have been omitted without any harm to the letter.]

Back to crass business. *Let me remind you again about the special Price-Reduction Offer, which is worth $10 to you if you accept it within 15 days. This offer reduces the price of your course to only $30.00, payable on terms of less than 17¢ a day.*

[A lot of money for 1925, but breaking it down to seventeen cents a day eases the pain considerably.]

A delightful closer: *After you read the enclosed booklet, and have tested your ability to correct the errors given in it, I feel sure that you will enroll for Mr. Cody's course—that you would enroll even without this special inducement. But there is no reason why you shouldn't have this saving.* DON'T LET THE DATE PASS WITHOUT ENROLLING. [No reason at all—a good way to turn a sow's ear into a silk purse. Restating an offer in a friendly, conversational way is insurance.]

An early version of today's buck slip adorns the back page of the letter: "A Special Personal Word from Sherwin Cody," who reminds the reader that "Each new day, your life has twenty-four hours less to run. Enroll now—it is the best thing you can do for yourself."

The Sherwin Cody Course is part of direct marketing history. With its justly celebrated headline "Do You Make These Mistakes in English?" its long-running ad harvested many, many inquiries. But the really hard job—converting those inquiries to sales—was done by uncompromising, tough letters that pounded home their message. It's easy to joke now about the hard sell in those yellowing, crumpling letters, but to today's direct mail practitioner, many of their lessons can be more valuable than the courses they were hawking.

Look It Up in the Encyclopaedia Britannica

From *The Encyclopaedia Britannica's* article on advertising *(11th edition, 1911):*

The fact that the verb "to circularize" was first used in 1848, sufficiently indicates the very recent origin of the practice of plying possible purchasers with printed letters and pamphlets. The penny postage was not established in England until 1840; the halfpenny post for circulars was not introduced until 1855. In the United States a uniform rate of postage at two cents was not established until 1883. In both countries cheap postage and cheap printing have so greatly encouraged the use of circulars that the sort of people whom the advertiser desires to reach—those who have the most money to spend, and whose addresses, published in directories, indicate their prosperous condition—are overwhelmed by tradesmen's price-lists, appeals from charitable institutions, and other suggestions for the spending of money. The addressing of envelopes and enclosing of circulars is now a recognized industry in many large towns both in Great Britain and in the United States. It seems, however, to be the opinion of expert advertisers that what is called "general circularizing" is unprofitable, and that circulars should only be sent to persons who have peculiar reason to be interested by their specific subject-matter. It may be noted, as an instance of the assiduity with which specialized circularizing is pursued, that the announcement of a birth, marriage or death in the newspapers serves to call forth a grotesque variety of circulars supposed to be adapted to the momentary needs of the recipient. . . .

What is called in England "postal trade," and in America "mail order business," is growing very rapidly. Small dealers in both countries have complained very bitterly of the competition they suffer from the general dealers and from stores made up of departments which, under one roof, offer to the consumer every imaginable sort of merchandise. This general trading, which, on the one hand, seriously threatens the small trader, and on the other hand offers greater possibilities of profit to the proportionately small number of persons who can undertake business on so large a scale, becomes infinitely more formidable when the general dealer endeavours not only to attract the trade of a town, but to make his place of business a centre from which he distributes by post his goods to remote parts of the country. In America, where the weight of parcels carried by post is limited to 4 lb., and where the private carrying companies are forced to charge a very much higher rate for carriage from New York to California than for shorter distances, the centralization of trade is necessarily limited; but it is no secret that, at the present moment, persons residing in those parts of the United Kingdom most remote from London habitually avail themselves of the English parcel post, which carries packages up to 11 lb., in order to procure a great part of their household supplies direct from general dealers in London. A trading company, which conducts its operations upon such a scale as this, can afford to spend an almost unlimited sum in advertising throughout the United Kingdom, and even the trader who offers only one specific class of merchandise is beginning to recognize the possibility of appealing to the whole country."

One "trader" who recognized rather early on "the possibility of appealing to the whole country" was *The Encyclopaedia Britannica* itself. On February 10, 1927, this sales letter was mailed from its New York City office:

Dear Sir:

The end of our Inventory Sale is now only a matter of days. Our stock of shopworn and demonstration sets is very nearly sold out and orders are being received at the rate of more than a hundred a day.

It seems as if nearly everyone to whom we sent our announcement wanted to take advantage of this unique opportunity.

As we explained previously, these sets are the genuine Thirteenth Edition, with guaranteed perfect text pages, the bindings being only very slightly worn. The present offer was made simply for the purpose of clearing them quickly from our inventory where of course they are classed as shopworn and demonstration sets. Actually they can hardly be distinguished from new sets that have been used for less than a fortnight.

At $79 for the Cloth binding these sets are probably the finest bargain we ever offered. It wasn't long ago when the only Britannica you could buy was the Cambridge Issue at $187. Now if you act promptly you can obtain one of these sets, the genuine Thirteenth Edition in the New form at a price which means a saving to you of more than $100. And you can pay for your set in small monthly amounts if you so desire.

Fifteen or twenty days at most will see the end of this sale. At any event, *this offer will be withdrawn March 4 and we reserve the right to return all orders received after our stock is exhausted even though they should be mailed before that date.*

I am putting the situation before you just as it stands because I believe you are really interested in this wonderful new edition of the Britannica. In fact we have sent this offer only to those who we believe would appreciate such a unique opportunity.

But we know that a bargain of this kind must clear out our few remaining sets in a very short time and we want you to have one of these sets if you are interested.

Remember—you will never get a better offer than this.

All you have to do is to fill out the enclosed card. You needn't send any money. You don't even have to look around for a stamp. The post card is stamped, ready for mailing. Choose your binding now, and see that your order is dropped in a mail box before the last collection tonight.

A letter filled with such delicious touches as "Fifteen or twenty days at most will see the end of this sale"—blending urgency with a quiet "literary" tone—and "I am putting the situation before you just as it stands"—being candid and newsy at the same time—is a blessedly human document.

The final call to action is a masterpiece: "You don't even have to look around for a stamp. The post card is stamped, ready for mailing. Choose your binding now, and see that your order is dropped in a mail box before the last collection tonight." No computer wrote *this* letter.

Is it possible to build a sales letter like this today, or is the statement that "you will never get a better offer than this" an instance of the clairvoyance of a 1927 direct mail copywriter?

Selling shopworn encyclopedias sixty years ago and selling, say, health insurance to credit-card holders today appear to be poles apart in terms of strategy and tactics. But the eternal harmonics of a stoutly constructed sales letter can bridge the years. The encyclopedia article on direct mail is a musty curio; the letter could still pull in orders tomorrow.

Another example of early *Encyclopaedia Britannica*–style direct mail is this two-pager on a 7 × 10½ sheet:

Dear Subscriber:

Christmas and Dickens and Plum Pudding go together. That is well understood wherever the time-honored traditions of this festive season are maintained.

And that is why we are now offering to our subscribers a unique opportunity.

This Christmas we want you to have the privilege to combine all three—the Christmas season, with

—the Complete Works of Charles Dickens

—and a genuine Fortnum & Mason English Plum Pudding, just the kind that Dickens used to relish so much.

(1) We have imported this special limited edition of the complete works of Charles Dickens from England where it was prepared under the supervision of Dickens' original publishers.

Printed in large readable type and bound in 22 volumes, this set is one of the finest in the market. And we can now offer it at a price which means a savings to you of $35.

You will be delighted with this fine authentic edition, which is illustrated with the original engravings by Phiz, Cruikshank, Leech, Seymour and other contemporaries of Dickens. Every true Dickens lover knows the value of the original illustrations executed under Dickens' supervision in harmony with the gay humor and picturesque quality of this text.

(2) The Plum Puddings have been imported by special order from Fortnum & Mason in Piccadilly (London), the very firm which supplied Dickens with Christmas plum puddings in his day. They are still made as they were in Dickens' time, "with rare mixings, matured to mellow perfection."

We shall take pleasure in presenting one of these masterpieces free with each set of Dickens while this offer lasts.

This offer is indeed unique. You have the opportunity of obtaining Dickens' Works in an edition that is authentic and complete, at the remarkably low price of $2.50 per volume, or $5.00 per month for twelve months if you wish to pay on the easy monthly terms. This is a special price made possible by a special purchase through our English office. The regular price of this edition would be $35 more.

Then, in addition, you get the delicious plum pudding FREE. This is a rare opportunity in itself, because these genuine Fortnum & Mason plum puddings are seldom imported to this country.

Both the Edition and the shipment of plum puddings are limited in number, so I must advise you to act promptly. This special Christmas offer is valid only until December 20. But the demand may easily exhaust our supply of sets and puddings long before that time (we have less than 500 of each).

Fill in the enclosed order form and mail it to us today. This will insure the delivery of your Dickens and your plum pudding in time for the celebration of Christmas Day. Send no money—we will bill you later.

Very sincerely yours,

Well . . . wasn't that a splendid Christmas letter! As sure-footed as a tiger moving toward its prey. Not a wasted word. Sensible, thrusting, with a great idea. The letter is dated November 17, 1926. It could have been written yesterday.

It's as rich as the plum puddings it celebrates—enough Dickensian references to stroke readers without distracting them, a nice savings, a good reason to act promptly, and no mention of the rather hefty total price (in 1926 dollars).

It could have been used to illustrate an article on direct mail in the *Encyclopaedia Britannica!*

Lessons From a Master: Robert Collier's Mail Order Course

Back in 1938, Robert Collier, one of the most important pioneers in direct mail, put together a mail order course on . . . mail order.

The three-page letter promoting this $28 service is classic Collier—hard-hitting, clear, and mouth-watering—and worth the price of admission in itself.

In all likelihood, Collier wrote the letter, although it's signed by "H. D. Parker, Registrar." It bears the trademarks that made him so successful: simplicity, earnestness, good sense, and a flow as powerful as the Colorado River. This is "whitewater" writing, and it won't let you off until it reaches its destination!

Garish though it may seem today, this single-spaced document hectographed or "spirit-duplicated" in purple ink with narrow margins really works hard, and is totally convincing.

A printed headline above the letterhead ("Economy Manuscript Publishers, 1229 Park Row Building, New York City, NY") reads:

Learn Collier's Secret of Turning the Tide of Riches in Your Favor, and Turning It NOW.

The superscription, or headline block above the salutation, sets the tone for the letter:

Here Is a True Story Which Gives the Secret of How to Get Rid of Money Worries For The Rest of Your Days!

Without hemming or hawing, Collier draws you immediately into his story—with an anecdote to "get the reader's attention and lead logically on to a description of your proposition."

Dear Reader:

Have you ever heard the story of the young telegraph operator in a crossroads country town who wanted to build an independent business of his own?

He had no money, and his salary was so small that he could hardly make ends meet. But he decided that he had to risk some of the scant salary if ever he was to get anywhere. So he bought $5 worth of postage stamps and then in his spare time penned letters to other telegraphers along the line, telling them about a low-priced watch he could get for them at a special price.

The next paragraph springs the "surprise"—that lowly telegrapher was Richard W. Sears.

"and his business today is known as Sears Roebuck & Company, the largest and most successful mail order house in the United States."

Such things could be done years ago . . . perhaps you will say . . . but there are no such opportunities today. You are wrong. There are little businesses springing up all over the country today. Right after a great depression always offers the finest opportunities. "You must show the reader how he is going to benefit."

Then follow several examples of successful mail order practitioners:

You have heard of John Blair of Warren . . . who borrowed $100 for the postage to mail his first 10,000 letters. You have heard of Davis of Gloucester, the man who sells fish by mail . . . he has sold as much as $2,000,000 worth of fish BY MAIL in a single year.

Examples and anecdotes fill one page. But now Collier shows a little steel (as he asks, "What will it do for the reader?"):

Yes, I have heard of all of these, you are probably thinking, but where do I come in? Let met ask you this: Have you ever wished that YOU could start a little business of your own and develop it to where it would bring YOU a nice income for the rest of your days? You have—of course—we all have. So here's where you come in.

Collier now proceeds to talk about himself:

There is here in New York a man named Robert Collier, who not only built a big business of his own by mail, but who has probably done more than anyone in the country today in building up business for others!

Collier is the man who started the sale by mail of the Harvard Classics. He sold several million dollars' worth of Well's Outline of History. He sold more than 100,000 Traveling Bags. He wrote a set of books on Practical Psychology—and got a million dollars' worth of orders for them by mail in a single year!

He sold oranges, grapefruits, candy . . . all by mail. His fees have run as high as $500 for a single letter.

And now this man has put all his experience . . . into one practical, usable course, that will show you HOW TO BUILD A BUSINESS OF YOUR OWN BY MAIL.

Several more paragraphs on how to raise money, collect it, how to sell by mail, and so on. Then a lovely paragraph:

Listen, my friend—let me sincerely say that if Collier can put into it only a tenth part of the skill and insight that have gone into his own campaigns, then every day you delay reading this Course, you are missing and heedlessly passing by something you have sought for years . . . the power of cashing in on your abilities . . . changing hope to HAVE.

Four paragraphs are devoted to a free examination offer, the cheapness of the course, and the necessity to get at least 1,000 subscribers:

To go to all this expense for any smaller number than 1,000 subscribers would necessitate sharing a far higher price for the Course . . . probably $50 to $100.

Then, the twist of the rapier:

Mind you, the enclosed form does not definitely commit you to take the course and pay $28 for it. It commits you only to send for the first lesson . . . when and if we notify you that we can accept your subscription. Will you mail the enclosed Reservation Sheet right away? If not mailed at once, it may be too late, for we need less than 300 additional subscribers, and when they are in, the subscription will be closed for this summer.

[Collier used to preach that "as the tail is to the kite, as the rudder is to the ship, so is the close to any important letter."] The order form, a simple 8½ × 11 sheet, instructs the Economy Manuscript Publishers that

"you may enter my application for the course of 15 lessons. I enclose first payment of $1 and agree to send you $2.25 each month until $28 has been paid you."

The really canny reader would have kept his money, for the sales letter itself was an excellent introduction to the world of mail order and powerful direct mail copy.

Take Your Lead From Direct Marketing Classics

After the Oldest Direct Mail Writer in the business marked his golden anniversary on the job, and then abruptly retired, a batch of fading files was found in his rolltop desk.

They were almost thrown out with the L. C. Smith manual typewriter, three quires of carbon paper, and a bottle of black ink, but fortunately one of the more history-minded younger writers asked the office manager if she might keep them.

This wise packrat now had the reputation for writing some of the brightest, most interesting leads in the business. Her secret: a swipe file dating back over a half century.

Let's look at some of the leads in the original letters and marvel at the ingenuity, brashness, and knowledge of what makes people buy that these early direct mail writers brought to every assignment:

I once figured that I throw into my wastebasket every year at least $50.00 worth of literature which people send me in the mistaken notion that I have nothing to do but read.

You are probably in the same situation.

—The Alexander Hamilton Institute, September 14, 1936

In order that you may realize at once the very unusual importance of this letter, let me tell you, before going into details, that we have secured a few special sets of one of the greatest library treasures of all time—almost unobtainable now in any of the original editions—and we can let you have one of these sets for less than one quarter of the former subscription price. But the sets we have will not go very far, and if you want one of them, you'll have to say so now.

—Funk & Wagnalls, February 1927

Before launching an extensive advertising campaign on our NEW WORLD LOOSE LEAF ATLAS, we are conducting some mail tests to ascertain the most responsive markets. As one of those selected in your community, you are, therefore, offered an exceptionally attractive opportunity, and we urge you to read over the enclosed circular very carefully.

—C. S. Hammond & Company, January 1930

More than thirty-two thousand of our Literary Digest subscribers have accepted our invitation to become members of The Society of Applied Psychology, upon our definite promise that they would greatly benefit physically, mentally, and financially.

—Literary Digest, September 1926

We are very glad to get your inquiry at this time because right now we are in a position to make you a very special offer on the New Improved Sharples Tubular Separator which is, in our judgment, the best separator ever made. And we are surely in a position to judge after 46 years of leadership in the separator industry.

—The Sharples Separator Co., January 26, 1928

Don't keep valuable papers, jewelry, or money in desk, table, or dresser drawers!

There's too much danger of loss, fire and theft.

The proper place for important documents, insurance policies, your will, personal correspondence, and money for current expenses is in the steel, fire and theft-resisting "My Safe" File.

May we send you one, postpaid, on a week's free approval, without your paying a penny?"

—New Process Company, 1932

This letter brings you the most astonishing offer that has ever been made in the distribution of the Historian's History of the World.

This is inventory time and we find we have on hand a certain number of shopworn and demonstration sets of the new Fifth Edition of the Historian's History. These sets are in excellent condition. The type pages are perfect! The bindings are no more worn than they would be after the books had been in your library for a few weeks.

But these demonstration sets cannot go back into our regular stock. They must be cleared out at once.

—Encyclopaedia Britannica, February 25, 1927

Now, while you are considering the REDUCED PRICE offer I made you—$45.50 less than others have paid—I wonder if you realize that—

YOU ARE PAYING FOR
YOUR N.S.T.A. TRAINING—
WITHOUT GETTING IT!

Yes sir—you are paying at the rate of $25.00 to $50.00 every week. When thousands of N.S.T.A. members earn $25.00 to $50.00 MORE

EVERY WEEK than they did before, you'll surely agree that by LEARNING SALESMANSHIP you can do as well or better and that you actually are paying for a training that you are not getting."

—National Salesman's Training Assn., March 9, 1932

This morning our Director of Extension Work referred your name to me, stating that he had written to you yesterday and that probably your enrollment blank would reach you in a few days, starting you as a student.

In order not to lose any time, I want to explain the Employment Service to you, and at the same time send you a blank to fill out for the Employment Department's file, so that we can find you Electrical work as soon as possible."

—National School of Visual Education, January 22, 1929

Old-Time Inspirations

"Ask yourself fairly—why slave, toil, grind along in a rut, making money for someone else—when you might as well devote your time, brains, labor, ambition for yourself? It is that freedom the mail order business confers. Thousands have proved it. So can you!"

—The Mail Order Dealer

During the 1920s, some 6,000 mail order people received *The Mail Order Dealer* every month.

Billing itself "America's Liveliest Mail Trade Journal," this forty-four page magazine was issued by the Gossip Printery of Holton, Kansas, as a mixed bag of inspiration, practical ideas, and ads that made snake-oil salesmen seem like models of restraint by comparison.

In the April 1928 issue, for instance, mail order dealers learned the answer to "The Most Frequently Asked Question That Arises in the Mail Order Business: How can I start a mail order business with $100 capital?"

The editor, just a little patronizingly, pointed out:

Before you can reasonably hope to carry on a traffic by mail in anything—or induce the public to send you its money—for anything—there are at least four items for which you must spend some money.

The first of these is service—service in planning your business, service in advising you intelligently and service in writing the matter and material you expect to use to go out and get business for you. It usually requires from $25 to $100 for that one thing alone.

Not content with shaking up the poor boob by revealing the exorbitant fees expected by a freelance copywriter, the editor laid down the law about printed matter.

Stationery, circulars, folders, booklets, form letters and the like cost money. A reasonably small quantity of such things will easily run up to a hundred dollars in cost.

By now, the would-be mail order mogul has decided to invest his $100 in a combination icebox and pocket watch repair shop, but the editor hasn't finished with him.

The third indispensable factor for which money must be spent from the absolute beginning is postage. Twenty dollars will buy 1,000 two-cent stamps, so you can easily see that if you mail out only 5,000 pieces of matter, your $100 is shot for postage stamps alone.

His bubble burst, the former entrepreneur turns to trudge dejectedly back to the family farm, but our editor keeps after him, contemptuously listing the snares and traps awaiting the unwary.

The fourth indispensable factor to take into consideration is advertising. Usually the mail order beginner makes the mistake of considering advertising first in his figuring—but that doesn't make it right to do so. Before you advertise at all you certainly should have your follow up in absolute readiness and complete, to handle the first inquiry that results from your advertising. To do otherwise is sheer waste. But advertising costs money. You cannot evade or avoid spending good hard cash for advertising if you expect to set up and operate a mail order business. To try and get along without it is exactly as sensible as it would be to buy a motor car, and then expect it to operate without ever spending a dime for gas.

Now the editor really lashes out at the simp, who is undoubtedly resolving never to ask advice from anyone again.

Possibly $100 would enable you to dabble a little in mail order, in a childish way, not expecting any cash returns, and, in fact no result but the slight satisfaction of your curiosity. The only really sensible thing to do with $100 is plant it in a savings bank somewhere and refuse to spend it till you have run it up to three or four or five or six hundred dollars. Then you have a reasonable chance for success in the mail order business. If you go stupidly along and squander your little cash capital, you certainly have nobody but yourself to blame if you lose it!

If the would-be mail order tycoon still refused to take the editor's advice, he was still able to invest his money in one of the schemes advertised in *The Mail Order Dealer*. For instance, for fifty cents he could receive a formula chart of sixteen beauty preparations, guaranteed up-to-date, or he could peddle the Bootlegger's Map of America. ("A scream and whirlwind selling sensation.") A Toledo, Ohio, chemist offered "another big seller in the toilet article line—Gloslay, a liquid hair dressing. This preparation supplies wonderful nourishment to the hair and scalp by applying it to the scalp and rubbing it in briskly. The materials that enter into this product cost about 50 cents a gallon."

But in between the fever-pitch articles and get-rich schemes in the ads, there were also plain-spoken articles that quietly offered help.

For instance, Fred G. Knell confided to his readers:

A simple mail order method that brought excellent results was the giving of "Unit Checks" with every 50 cents worth of goods sold— 20 of these checks returned (showing that the customer had purchased $10 worth of goods) entitled him to one dollar in cash.

This, you see, was really only a 10 percent discount, but worked in the manner suggested; it was certainly a fine little trade winner.

Raymond G. Schmitt gave the readers of his article on "How to write business-building sales letters" two "first class attention-attracting opening sentences":

To show you my confidence in the book—(saying nothing about my confidence in you)—I will send you a copy of it by parcel post, charges prepaid, upon receipt of your order and remittance of only 50 cents.

Answer this one question—Did my stenographer type this letter to you personally on her machine—or is it a form letter?

And C. D. Craddock told his readers all about "The Ad Writer and His Clients" in an article that could have been written yesterday:

> If you have occasion to employ the services of an advertising writer, by all means be fair. Do not accept too literally statements to the effect that copy will bring you all the results you want. From a business standpoint, a good advertising writer is justified in claiming that his copy will produce results. He'd be a poor advertising writer not to advertise his own business and efficiency. But an honest and reliable advertising writer does not expect his copy to open the gates of prosperity for you and he cannot guarantee that it will. He has reason to believe, though, that his material will help you possibly far beyond your expectations if you operate your business properly, efficiently and intelligently and use copy the way it is intended to be.

Collection Letters From the Depression Era

There have probably been more changes in direct marketing in the last five years than in the previous seventy-five, thanks to the computer, more sophisticated marketing techniques, new media, and new marketplaces. In our impatience to win control over this mushrooming business, we sometimes tend to reinvent the wheel, ignoring the efforts of those who came before us.

But direct marketing has a long history, and it can be profitable to examine some of the lessons learned in the past, and perhaps even put some of the old wine into new bottles.

Take collection letters. Well, in the old days, laws were a lot more lenient. You could say things that would not be countenanced today. But a lot of ingenuity was still required to get people to pay their debts and still keep their business.

In 1931, for instance, the Imperial Candy Company of Seattle found itself with 500 past-due accounts. Times were tough and the candy company was finding collections difficult. So the following letter, over the signature of the president, was sent out:

Dear _____:

It is usually considered difficult to write letters about money, but I don't think there is any need for hesitation in times like these. Fairness and frankness on both sides will always avoid any misunderstanding.

As you know, your account with us is overdue. The times call for the fullest cooperation. If you need it you will find us ready to go the limit of our resources to assist you over the rough spots.

At the same time, you will appreciate that we have many dealers on our books and that we cannot give extended unlimited time. Our problem is just the same as yours—we have to meet our obligations, payrolls, etc.

If you can send us a check now it will help us mightily. If you simply cannot at this time, a note from you telling when it would be convenient will be greatly appreciated. We are vitally interested in keeping the credit of every one of our dealer-friends in good standing.

Won't you let us hear from you either with a payment or with an explanation of the situation so that we can help you to meet your problem to the best advantage of both of us?

Sincerely yours,

Soon after the letter was in mail, the response started. One dealer drove forty miles to bring $25.00 in person (this was, after all, 1931, and $25.00 was a lot of money). Another dealer, with a sheepish grin, handed a check for $179.50 to an Imperial salesman. "That letter I got from your boss made me feel pretty cheap."

The response rate? More than 50 percent. There were probably six good reasons for this success:

1. Sending it over the president's signature tended to obtain for it more than ordinary attention.
2. It goes directly to the point without any attempt at cleverness, wit, or humor.
3. It acknowledged the hard times and so took the sting out of the request for money.
4. It offered complete cooperation to the dealer willing to explain his own situation.
5. It created a bond of sympathetic understanding, by establishing a shared business problem.
6. And, very tactfully, it hinted in the sentence "We are vitally interested in keeping the credit of every one of our dealer-friends in good standing" that lack of response might lead to impaired credit.

Another Depression collection letter was the one used in 1933 by Porter-Cable-Hutchinson Corporation, a maker of industrial equipment.

Dear _____:

Do you remember the time when your mother sent you downtown with a little red string around your finger to act as a reminder of what you were to do? It was a lifesaver sometimes, wasn't it?

Well, this letter, like the little red string, is to remind you of something. Don't forget that your October account for $_____ is overdue and that we are expecting your check for it in a very few days.

Sincerely yours,

There's a warm friendliness about this very short letter, with the charming little picture painted in the first paragraph segueing naturally into the plea for settlement in the second.

And in 1948, this letter was offered as a good example of a collection note that was fair, courteous, and considerate:

Dear————:

The fellows who coined the expressions that "Silence is golden" and that "No news is good news" certainly weren't credit men. They couldn't have been!

To those whose job it is to keep the wheels of credit turning smoothly, the customer's cooperation in the payment of his account means a great deal.

But now and then a payment is unavoidably delayed by something unexpected. We understand how this can happen; and when it does, we always try to meet the customer halfway in solving the problem.

So won't you help us to come our half of the way? If you can't send us your check for $———— just now, please tell us what we can do to help. If you need a little more time on this bill, just let us know, for we really want to cooperate.

Sincerely yours,

Some dicta that were laid down in a trade magazine article on collection letters in the late 1940s still hold true:

1. Avoid curt statements that will irritate the reader. Example: "If you cannot pay this bill at once, let us know when you can."
2. Give your letter a *human* tone.
3. Keep your letter short. No one enjoys reading any collection letter, let alone a long one.
4. Don't sound annoyed or exasperated.
5. Ask for the money or close with a statement that stimulates action.

And a 1925 commentator on collection letters noted:

Every good collection man of my acquaintance is constantly on the hunt for new ideas. And usually the seemingly new idea, when he finds it, isn't really new. It turns out to be only a new form of an idea that's old. The new collection letter usually contains the same old appeal. All that has been done has been to find a new form of expression.

And sometimes those new forms of expression can be found in old letters.

Index